W9-AAA-785

5

Show What You Know® on the
COMMON CORE

Assessing Student Knowledge of the Common Core State Standards
(CCSS)

Reading
Mathematics

Name:

Published by:

Show What You Know® Publishing
A Division of Englefield & Associates, Inc.
P.O. Box 341348
Columbus, OH 43234-1348
Phone: 614-764-1211
www.showwhatyouknowpublishing.com

Standards are from the Common Core State Standards Initiative Website at www.corestandards.org dated 2011.

Printed in the United States of America
13   12   11   20 19 18 17 16 15 14 13 12 11 10 9 8 7 6 5 4 3 2 1

ISBN: 1-59230-456-7

Acknowledgements

Show What You Know® Publishing acknowledges the following for their efforts in making this assessment material available for students, parents, and teachers:

Cindi Englefield, President/Publisher
Eloise Boehm-Sasala, Vice President/Managing Editor
Jennifer Harney, Editor/Illustrator

About the Contributors

The content of this book was written BY teachers FOR teachers and students and was designed specifically for the Common Core State Standards for Grade 5. Contributions to the Reading and Mathematics sections of this book were also made by the educational publishing staff at Show What You Know® Publishing. Dr. Jolie S. Brams, a clinical child and family psychologist, is the contributing author of the Test Anxiety and Test-Taking Strategies chapters of this book. Without the contributions of these people, this book would not be possible.

Table of Contents

Introduction

Dear Student:

This *Show What You Know® on the Common Core for Grade 5, Student Workbook* was created to give you lots of practice in preparation for your state proficiency test in Reading and Mathematics.

The first two chapters in this workbook—Test Anxiety and Test-Taking Strategies—were written especially for fifth-grade students. Tackling Test Anxiety offers advice on how to get rid of the bad feelings you may have about tests. The Test-Taking Strategies chapter gives you examples of the kinds of questions you will see on the test and includes helpful tips on how to answer these questions correctly so you can succeed on all tests.

The next two chapters of this Student Workbook help you prepare for the Reading and Mathematics test.
- The Reading chapter includes two full-length Reading Assessments and a Reading Glossary of Terms that will help you show what you know.

- The Mathematics chapter includes two full-length Mathematics Assessments, a Glossary of Mathematics Terms, and a Glossary of Mathematical Illustrations that will help you show what you know.

This Student Workbook will provide a chance to practice your test-taking skills to show what you know.

Good luck!

This page intentionally left blank.

Tackling Test Anxiety

Worry Less about Tests

Lots of students worry about taking tests, so, if you are a test worrier, you are not alone! Many of your classmates and friends also have fearful feelings about tests, but they usually do not share their feelings. Keeping feelings to yourself is not a good idea because it just makes things worse. You may feel you are the only person with a problem and there is no one out there to help, but that is not true. Be brave! When you talk to your parents, teachers, and friends about your test-taking worries, you will feel better. You will find out that other people (even your teachers and parents) have felt worried, nervous, or scared about taking tests. You will then have other people on your team to battle the test monster.

When students feel nervous, worried, and scared, it sometimes seems there is no way out. This is also not true! Everyone can feel calm about taking tests. You don't have to be the smartest student, the most popular kid, or the fastest athlete to be a brave test taker. You just need to be willing to try; you will be amazed at how much better you will feel.

What is it Like to Have Test Anxiety?

One definition of the word anxiety is feeling anxious, worried, and scared. When students feel this way about taking tests, it is called test anxiety. In this chapter, the phrase "test anxiety" will be used a lot. Just remember that no matter what you call it, you will learn how to beat the test monster.

All sorts of students have test anxiety. It doesn't matter if a student is tall or short, shy or friendly, or a girl or a boy. Students with test anxiety might be different in a lot of ways, but they have many of the same thoughts and feelings about taking tests. Here are some of the ways students with test anxiety think and feel:

- **Students who have test anxiety don't think good things about themselves.**
  Instead of thinking about all they know, these students spend most of their time thinking about what they don't know. When their minds become filled with lists of what they don't know, there isn't any

room left for remembering what they have learned and all they can do. It is like their minds are closets filled with only bad things, never good ones. Imagine if you filled your closet at home with broken toys, worn-out clothes, crumpled-up papers, and all sorts of garbage. You would open up your closet and say to yourself, "Boy, my life is awful!" You would ignore all the other good things you might have in your room, as well as in your life. You can bet you would not be feeling very good about yourself.

- **Students who have test anxiety exaggerate.**
  Exaggerating means making things bigger than they are. While exaggeration makes books and movies exciting and interesting, exaggeration makes test anxiety worse. Worried thoughts grow like a mushroom out of control. "Oh no! I don't know how to do this type of math problem. See, I can't do anything! I am the worst math student ever, and I'm sure my life will be a total mess!" Students with test anxiety make the worst out of situations and imagine all kinds of things that will not really happen. Their thoughts get scarier and scarier, and their futures look darker and darker. The more these students exaggerate, the more anxious and worried they become.

- **Students who have test anxiety sometimes do not feel well.**
  It is important to remember your mind and body work together. What goes on in your mind can change how your body feels, and how your body feels can change what goes on in your thinking. When your mind is filled with worries about tests, your body may also worry. You may feel your heart jumping, your stomach might hurt, your hands might become sweaty, your head may hurt, or you might even feel that you can't breathe very well. Feeling bad gets in the way of doing your best on tests. Feeling bad also makes students feel even more anxious. They say to themselves, "My heart is really beating fast, and my hands are shaking. See, I'm such a mess; I'll fail that test!" Then, they just become more worried and more anxious. Some students with test anxiety miss a lot of school, not because they are lazy, but because they believe they really are not feeling well. Sadly, the more school they miss, the more they fall behind, and the more nervous they feel. Their physical feelings keep them from enjoying school and facing the test monster.

- **Students who have test anxiety want to escape.**
  When some students are anxious, they feel so bad that they will do anything to stay away from that feeling. They run away from problems, especially tests. Some students try to get away from tests by missing school or maybe by going to the nurse's office. This does not solve any problems because the more a student is away from the classroom, the harder the school work becomes. In the end, students who try to get away feel even worse than they did before, and they will have to take the test later on anyway. Running away from problems that cause anxiety may seem to make you feel better for a while, but it does not solve problems or make them go away.

- **Students who have test anxiety do not show what they know on tests.**
  For students who are feeling worried and anxious, it's really hard to make good decisions. Instead of concentrating on the test, planning out their answers, and using what they know, students who have test anxiety blank out. They stare at the paper and see that no answer is there. They become stuck and cannot move on. Some students come up with the wrong answer because their worries get in the way of reading directions carefully or thinking about their answers. Their minds are running in a hundred different directions, and none of those directions seems to be getting them anywhere. They forget to use what they know, and they also forget to use study skills that would help them do their best. Imagine your mind as a safe. Inside the safe are all the answers to tests and a whole lot of knowledge about school work. However, anxiety has taken away the key. Even though the answers are there, the key is gone. Your mind is racing, and you can't think clearly about where you put the key! All that knowledge is trapped in there with nowhere to go. When students feel calmer about taking tests, their wonderful minds open up, and exciting ideas come pouring out.

Are You One of These Test Anxious Fifth Graders?

As you have seen, students with test anxiety think bad things about themselves, feel sick some of the time, and forget how to do well on tests. Do any of the kids described below remind you of yourself?

Stay-Away Stephanie

Stephanie's thoughts tell her it is better to stay away from anything that might be hard to do: especially tests. Stephanie is a good girl, but she is always in trouble for trying to avoid tests. Sometimes, Stephanie will beg her mother to allow her to stay home on test days. When that doesn't work, she will refuse to get out of bed or to catch the bus to school. You'd better believe she gets in trouble for that! Sometimes, at school, she will hide in the bathroom or go to the school nurse when test-taking time comes. Stephanie truly believes there is nothing worse than taking a test. She has so much anxiety that she forgets about all the problems that will happen when she stays away from her responsibilities. Stay-Away Stephanie feels less nervous when she stays away from tests, but she never learns to face her fears.

Worried Wendy

Wendy is the type of fifth grader who always looks for the worst thing to happen. Her mind is filled with all types of worried thoughts. She exaggerates everything bad and forgets about everything good. Her

mind races a mile a minute with all sorts of thoughts and ideas about tests, all of them bad. The more she thinks, the worse she feels, and then her problems become huge. Instead of just worrying about a couple of difficult questions on a test, she finds herself thinking about failing the whole test, being made fun of by her friends, being grounded by her parents, and never going to college. She completely forgets that her parents are really nice and not strict, her friends like her for a whole bunch of reasons, and doing poorly on one test is not going to ruin her life. Wendy is always watching and waiting for the worst thing to happen. She spends her time worrying instead of figuring out how to do well.

Critical Chris

Chris is the type of fifth grader who spends all of his time putting himself down. No matter what happens, he always feels he has failed. While some people hold grudges against others, Chris holds grudges against himself. Even if he makes little mistakes, he can never forget them. Chris has had many good things happen in his life, and he has been successful many times. Unfortunately, Chris forgets the good and only remembers the bad. If he gets a "C+" on a test, he can't remember the times he earned an "A" or a "B." When he gets a "B+" on a test, he says to himself, "I made a lot of stupid mistakes, so I didn't get an 'A.'" He never compliments himself by thinking, "I did AWESOME by getting a 'B+.'" If Chris liked himself better, he would have less test anxiety.

Victim Vince

Most fifth graders know it is important to take responsibility for themselves, but Vince wants to blame everything on others. He can't take responsibility for himself at all. He thinks everything is someone else's fault and constantly complains about friends, parents, school work, and especially about tests. He thinks his teachers are unfair and life is against him. Vince does not feel there is anything he can do to prepare for the state proficiency test or to help himself in any other way. Because he does not try to learn test-taking skills or understand why he is afraid, he just keeps feeling angry, sad, and worried.

Perfect Pat

Every fifth grader needs to try his or her best, but no one should try as much as Pat! Pat studies and studies, and when she is not studying, she is worrying. No matter what she does, it's never enough. She will write book reports over and over and will study for tests until she is exhausted. Trying hard is fine, but, no matter what Pat does, she feels she has not done enough. She feels worried because she cannot stop thinking there is always more to know. Her anxiety gets higher and higher, but this does not mean she does better and better on tests. In fact, the more anxious she gets, the harder tests become. Then, when she does not do well on a test, she just wants to study more and more. What a mess! Pat should spend more time learning how to study and find time to relax.

How Can I Feel Calmer about Tests?

Test anxiety is a very powerful feeling that makes students feel they are weak and helpless. Nervous feelings can be so powerful that it sometimes seems there is nothing you can do to stop them. Worries seem to take over your mind and body and leave you feeling like you are going to lose the test-anxiety battle for sure.

The good news is that there are many things you can do to win the battle over test anxiety. If you can learn these skills in elementary school, you are on the road to success in middle school and for all the other challenges in your life.

- **Don't let yourself feel alone.**
  Although sometimes it is fun to curl up in bed and read a book by yourself, most of the time it is not very much fun to be alone. This is really true when you are feeling anxious or worried. Talking to your friends, parents, and teachers about worried feelings, especially feelings about test taking, can really help you feel better. Having test-taking worries does not mean there is something wrong with you. You might be surprised to find out that many of your friends and classmates also feel anxious about tests. You might even be more surprised to learn that your parents and teachers also had test anxiety when they were younger. They know what you are going through and are there to help you.

- **There is more than one side to any story.**

  Most fifth graders have heard a parent or teacher tell them, "There is more than one side to any story." It is easy to get in the habit of thinking about situations in a bad way instead of thinking happy thoughts. You can help yourself feel better about your life and about taking tests by training yourself to think about things from a happy point of view.

  Think about a can of soda pop. Get out a piece of paper and a pen or pencil. Now, draw a line down the middle of the paper. On one side, write the heading "All the bad things about this can of soda pop." On the other side of the paper, write the heading "All the good things about this can of soda pop." Fill in the chart with your thoughts about the can of soda pop. When you are finished, your chart might look like the one below.

All the bad things about this can of soda pop	All the good things about this can of soda pop
Not an attractive color	Easy-to-read lettering
It's getting warm	Nice to have something to drink
Not much in the can	Inexpensive
Has a lot of sugar	Recyclable aluminum cans

Look how easy it is to write down either good things or bad things about a silly can of soda pop. That can of soda pop is not good or bad; it's just a can of soda pop. You can either look at it in a good way, or you can think about everything bad that comes to your mind. Doesn't the same thing hold true for tests? Tests are not good or bad in themselves. Tests are just a way to challenge you and to see how much you know. Studying for tests can be boring and can take up a lot of free time, but you can also learn a lot when you study. Studying can make you feel great about yourself. Even if you make some mistakes on a test, you can learn from those mistakes. You can also look at your test results and compliment yourself on how much you have learned. The way you think about tests has a lot to do with how well you will be able to "show what you know." Students who have good thoughts about tests are less anxious and do better. Students who always have bad thoughts and feelings about tests usually do not do as well as they should.

- **Think good things about yourself!**

The better you feel about yourself, the better you will do on tests. This does not mean you should go around boasting and bragging to your friends about how wonderful you are! What helps most on tests is to think about all the good things you have done and learned in your past. Remind yourself of those things when you are studying for tests or even when you are taking a test.

Thinking good things about yourself takes practice. The chart below is divided into three parts. For the first part, fill in as many sentences as you can that describe "Why I Am Special." In the example below, this fifth grader has already filled in "I am very kind to animals" and "I have a good sense of humor." Next, you want to remember what you have done in your life. Make a section on the chart that reads "Things I Have Done." The fifth grader below has started his chart by remembering "I helped paint my room" and "I got a library award." Don't forget to ask your family to remind you about who you are and what you have done. Make believe you are a news reporter working on a story. Interview your parents, grandparents, aunts, uncles, brothers, sisters, or anyone else who can remind you of all the good things you have done and the good person you are. Make sure to add those to your chart. This fifth grader's grandfather told him he is "smiley." Keep a chart like this in a special place where you can look at it if you are feeling anxious about tests or not very good about yourself. Reading it will make you feel better. When you feel good about yourself or when something good happens, add it to the chart. You will be amazed at what a wonderful person you are. The better you feel about yourself, the better you will be able to show what you know in school and on tests.

Why I Am Special	Things I Have Done	What My Family Thinks
I am very kind to animals. I have a good sense of humor.	I helped paint my room. I got a library award.	Grandpa thinks I'm "smiley."

- **Everything is not a disaster!**
  If you always think a disaster is about to happen, it is called "catastrophizing." A catastrophe is a disaster. It is when something terrible happens. When students catastrophize about tests, their minds go on and on thinking about terrible scenes of failure. It is like a horror movie about school, but it is worse. It is real life!

  When students stop themselves from catastrophizing, their test anxiety becomes much less noticeable. When you feel yourself catastrophizing, make yourself stop. Tell yourself, "STOP! None of this is going to happen. Tests might be hard, but they are not going to be the end of the world." Disasters have a way of getting out of hand, so the sooner you can stop yourself thinking those thoughts, the better off you will be. Disaster thoughts get you nowhere; they only make you more anxious. The most important part is that they are not true! No matter how you do on tests in the fifth grade, your life will go on, and it will be just fine.

- **Don't make "should" statements.**
  Students make themselves anxious when they think they "should" do everything. They feel they should be as smart as everyone else, they should study more, and they should not feel anxious about tests. All of those thoughts are pretty ridiculous! Not everyone is going to be as smart as the next person, and you do not have to study until you drop to do well on tests. Instead of kicking yourself for not being perfect, it is better to set some reasonable goals about studying and school work. This will help you get better grades on tests and feel happier in your life.

- **Take out those bad thoughts and put in good ones!**
  If you are thinking good thoughts, it's impossible to think bad ones! People who are worried or anxious can become happier and more relaxed by thinking good thoughts. Even when something scary is happening, such as a visit to the dentist, thinking positive thoughts is very helpful. If you are thinking about something that is good or positive, it is almost impossible to think of something that is bad or negative. Keep this in mind when test anxiety starts to become a bother.

Try using some of these thoughts when you find yourself becoming worried:

Thoughts of success—Thinking "I can do it" thoughts chases away thoughts of failure. Imagining times when you were successful, such as doing well in a soccer game or figuring out a complicated brain teaser, will help you realize you can be successful. On the morning of the test, think positive thoughts. Think about arriving at school and feeling sure that you will do well on the test. Imagine closing your eyes before the test, breathing deeply, relaxing, and remembering all that you have learned. When you think about success, you will achieve success! During the test, remind yourself that you have been successful in the past and can do well in the future and on this test. This will chase away your worried thoughts.

Relaxing thoughts—You can't be worried and relaxed at the same time. Thinking about a time when you felt comfortable and happy can chase away your worries. Think about a time that you went swimming, had a pillow fight at a sleep over, or went out with your family for a huge ice cream sundae. Soon, you will find yourself thinking about the good things in life, not the worries that trouble you.

Thoughts about beating the test monster—When you get ready to take a test, imagine you are in battle with an ugly test monster! Think about the hard work that you do to study and the good things about yourself. Imagine there are huge swords chasing away the test monster. Imagine the test monster running for his life as you chase away your worries and show what you know on the test! Even though it might sound silly, it works!

- **Relaxing helps chase away anxiety.**

Just as you can calm your mind, it is also important for you to relax your body. When you have test anxiety, your muscles can become stiff. In fact, your whole body might become tense. Taking deep breaths before a test and letting them out slowly as well as relaxing muscles in your body are very helpful ways to feel less anxious. You may find that not only does relaxation help you on tests, but it is also helpful for other challenging situations and for feeling healthy overall. Athletes, astronauts, and surgeons all use relaxation to help them perform their best. Here are some other methods you can try. You might also discover a different method that works well for you. Some methods will work better than others for you, so be sure to use the methods that are best for you.

Listen to music—It probably doesn't matter what type of music you listen to as long as it makes you feel good about yourself. You might want to listen to music while you study, but if it disturbs your concentration, it will not be helpful. Listening to music when you go to sleep the night before a test or in the morning while you get ready for school may also help you relax.

Develop a routine—Some people find it relaxing to have a set routine to go through each morning. Having a calm morning and a nice breakfast before you take a test is always helpful. Rushing around on the morning of a test not knowing what to do next is only going to make your worries worse! When students rush and feel out of control, they begin to think, "I'll never get everything done," and, "This day is starting out terribly!" Ask your family to be respectful of your routine and tell them how they can help you be more successful. This might include giving you an extra hand in getting ready the morning of the test or making sure you get to school on time.

Take care of yourself—Everyone is busy. Most fifth graders are involved in all sorts of activities including sports, music, and helping around the house. They also love their free time and can stay out for hours skateboarding or just hanging around with their friends. Sometimes, they are so busy they forget to eat breakfast or they don't get enough sleep. Eating and sleeping right are important, especially before a test. Even if you are not a big breakfast eater, try to find something that you like to eat, and get in the habit of eating breakfast. When you do not eat right, you feel shaky, you have a hard time thinking, and you have more anxiety. Being tired does not help either. Try to get in the habit of going to bed early enough every night so that you feel fresh and rested for tests in school. Your body will be more relaxed if it is well-fed and well-rested.

Practice relaxing your body—No matter what method of relaxation you find works best for you, it is very important to practice that method so you feel comfortable with it. Practicing your relaxation method will help you during times when you are anxious because you will know what to do to calm yourself without having to worry about it; it will become your natural response to the stressful things around you.

- **Learn to use study skills.**
  There is a chapter in this book that will help you learn test-taking strategies. The more you know about taking tests successfully, the calmer you will feel. Knowledge is power! Practice test-taking strategies to reduce your test anxiety.

- **Congratulate yourself during the test.**
  Instead of thinking, "I've only done five problems, and I have so many pages to go," or, "I knew three answers, but one mixed me up," think about how well you have done so far. Tell yourself, "I've gotten some answers right, so I bet I can do more." If you concentrate on the good things you are doing during a test, you will stay calm and allow yourself to do more good things on that test.

- **Don't get down on yourself for feeling a little worried.**
  You are not alone if you feel worried about tests; everyone feels a little worried about tests. Don't be hard on yourself! If you keep telling yourself, "I'm worried, so I'll never do well," then the worst will probably happen. Instead, tell yourself, "Lots of kids get anxious. Let me just calm myself down, and I will do fine." It is important to remember that being a little worried is natural. If you know that worrying happens to everyone, it will help you defeat your anxiety and become calm and focused on the test you are taking. Remember, you are not alone in your test-taking worries.

Copying is Prohibited
© Englefield & Associates, Inc.

Test-Taking Strategies

You Can Do Your Best on Tests!

Most students want to do their best on tests. Tests are an important way for teachers to know how well students are doing and for students to understand how much progress they are making in school. Your state proficiency test helps schools find out how well students are learning. This helps teachers and principals make their schools even better. You can do the best job possible in showing what you know by learning how to be a good test taker.

It is not possible to do a good job without the right tools. Test-taking strategies are tools to help you show what you know on tests. Everyone needs good tools to fix a problem. It doesn't matter whether the problem is taking a test or fixing a broken bicycle; without good tools, it's hard to be a success. Think about what would happen if your bicycle breaks and you do not have the right tools to fix it. You might know a lot about bicycles, but you can't show what you know unless you have the correct tools to fix it. You might know that the bolts on your wheels have to be put on very tight, but how can you do that without good tools to help?

Tools are not tricks. Using good test-taking strategies is not cheating. The best students are not geniuses; they have learned to use good test-taking strategies. They learned what they need to do to show what they know when they are taking tests. You can learn these test-taking strategies, too!

Test-Taking Tools That You Can Use!

Be an active learner.

You might have heard the comment, "He soaks up knowledge like a sponge." Actually, the opposite of that idea is true. Although sponges soak up a lot of water just by lying around, your brain does not work that way with information. Just because you are sitting in a classroom does not mean you are going to learn anything simply by being there. Students learn when they participate during the school day. This is called active learning. Active learners pay attention to what is being said. They ask themselves questions about what they hear. Active learners enjoy school, learn a lot, feel good about themselves, and usually do better on tests.

It takes time and practice to become an active learner. If you are the type of student who is easily bored or always frustrated, it is going to take some practice to use your classroom time differently. Ask yourself the following questions.

- Do I look at the teacher when he or she is talking?

- Do I pay attention to what is being said?

- Do I have any questions or ideas about what the teacher is saying?

- Do I listen to what my classmates are saying and think about their ideas?

- Do I work with others to try to solve difficult problems?

- Do I look at the clock and wonder what time school will be over, or do I enjoy what is happening during the school day and wonder how much I can learn?

- Do I think about how my school work might help me now or in the future?

The more you actively participate in school, the more you will learn and the better you will do on tests. Think about Kristen!

There was a young girl named Kristen,
Who was bored and wouldn't listen.
She didn't train
To use her smart brain
And never knew what she was missing!

Do not rely on luck.

Although sometimes it's fun to believe in luck, luck alone is not going to help you do well on the state proficiency test or other tests. You might know a student who feels better having a lucky coin in his or her pocket or wearing a lucky pair of shoes when taking a test. That is fine, but the best way to do well on a test is to take responsibility for yourself by taking the time and effort to do well. It is easy to say to yourself, "It's not my fault that I did poorly. It's just not my lucky day." If you believe in luck and not in your own skills, you aren't going to get very far! Students who feel they have no control over what happens to them usually receive poor grades and do not do well on tests. Don't be like Chuck!

There was a cool boy named Chuck,
Who thought taking tests was just luck.
He never prepared.
He said, "I'm not scared."
When his test scores appear, he should duck!

Do your best every day!

Fifth grade is not an easy year. All of a sudden, the work seems really hard! Fifth-grade teachers are getting their students ready for middle school and are giving them more responsibility (and probably a lot more homework!). Sometimes, it feels like you will never learn all you need to know to do well on the state proficiency test. Many students begin to feel hopeless, and sometimes it seems easy just to give up.

Students are surprised when they find out that, if they just set small goals for themselves, they can learn an amazing amount! Do you know that if you learn just one new fact every day of the year, at the end of the year, you will know 365 new facts? Think about what happens if you learn three new facts every day. At the end of the year, you will have learned 1,095 new facts. When you think about the state proficiency test or other tests that you have to take in school, try to think about what you can learn step by step and day by day. If you try every day, you will be surprised at how all of this learning adds up to make you one of the smartest fifth graders ever. Think about Ray!

There was a smart boy named Ray,
Who learned something new every day.
He was pretty impressed
With what his mind could possess.
His excellent scores were his pay!

Get to know the test.

Most fifth graders are probably pretty used to using their own CD players, televisions, or alarm clocks. They know how to use all of the controls to get the loudest sound, the clearest picture, or the early wake up. Now, imagine you are asked to use some electronic equipment that you have never seen before. You would probably think to yourself, "Where is the volume control? How do I put channels in memory? I don't even know how to change the channels to begin with! How do I put the battery in this thing?" You would probably spend a lot of time trying to figure out how everything works.

Now, think about your state proficiency test. It will be very hard to do a good job if you've never seen that test before. Although your state proficiency test is a test, it is probably different from tests you have taken before. Getting to know the test is a great test-taking tool. The more you get used to the types of questions and how to record your answers, the better you will do. You will also save yourself time, time you can use to answer the questions instead of trying to understand how they work. Think about Sue!

There was a kid named Sue,
Who thought her test looked new.
"I never saw this before!
How'd I get a bad score?"
If she practiced, she might have a clue!

Read the directions and questions carefully!

Most fifth graders think directions are pretty boring. Fifth graders have already been in school for at least six years. Many of them think they have heard every direction ever invented, and it is easy for them to "tune out" directions. Not paying careful attention to the question that is being asked is a very bad idea. Do not tell yourself, "These directions are just like other directions I've had many times before," or, "I'm not really going to take time to read these directions because I know what the question will be." The directions on tests are not there to trick or to confuse you, but you cannot do well on this test if you do not read the directions and questions carefully. Read the directions and questions slowly. Repeat them to yourself. Ask yourself if what you are reading makes sense. These are powerful test-taking strategies. Think about Fred!

There was a nice boy named Fred,
Who forgot almost all that he read.
The directions were easy,
But he said, "I don't need these."
He should have read them instead.

Know how to fill in those answer bubbles.
By the time you are in the fifth grade, you have probably filled in answer bubbles on tests before. Remember, if you don't fill them in correctly, your answer will not be counted. Don't forget that a computer will be reading your answers. If you do not fill in the answer bubble dark enough, or if you use a check mark or dot, your smart thinking will not be counted! Look at the examples given below.

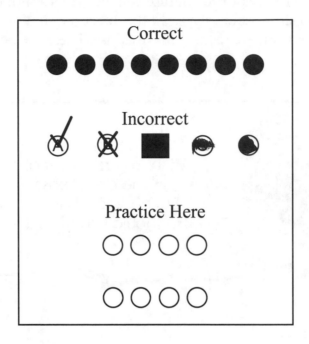

Learning how to fill in answer bubbles just takes a little practice. It may not be how you are used to writing answers, but it is one way to give a right answer on your state proficiency test. Think about Kay!

A stubborn girl named Kay
Liked to answer in her own way.
Her marked answer bubbles
Gave her all sorts of troubles.
Her test scores ruined her day!

Speeding through the test does not help!

Your state proficiency test gives students enough time to read and to answer all the questions. There will always be some students who finish the test more quickly than others, but this does not mean their scores will be better. It does not matter whether you finish quickly or slowly. As long as you take your time, prepare for the test, pay attention to the test, and use some of the skills you have learned in this book, you should do just fine. No one will get a better score just because he or she finishes first. Speeding through a test question or racing through the whole test does not help you do well. In fact, students do their best when they work carefully, not too slow and not too fast. Think about Liz!

There was a fifth grader named Liz,
Who sped through her test like a whiz.
She thought she should race,
At a very fast pace,
But it caused her to mess up her quiz.

Answer every question!

Did you know there is no penalty for guessing on your state proficiency test? That is really good news! That means you have a one out of four chance of getting a multiple-choice question right, even if you just close your eyes and guess. For every four questions you guess, you probably will get 25% (one out of four) of the questions right. This means it is better to guess than to leave questions blank. Guessing by itself is not going to make you a star on the test, but leaving multiple-choice questions blank is not going to help you either.

It is always better to study hard and be prepared, but everyone has to guess at some time or another. Some people do not like to guess because they are afraid of choosing the wrong answer, but there is nothing wrong with guessing if you can't figure out the correct answer. Think about Jess!

There was a smart girl named Jess,
Who thought it was useless to guess.
If a question was tough,
She just gave up.
This only added to her stress.

Some students use codes to help them make good answer choices. Using your pencil in the test booklet, you can mark the following codes next to each multiple-choice question. This will help you decide what answer will be best. It will even help you to guess! Read through the codes below.

(+)   Putting a "plus sign" by a choice means you think that choice is more correct than others.
(?)   Putting a "question mark" by a choice means you are not sure if that is the correct answer, but it could be. You don't want to rule it out completely.
(–)   Putting a "minus sign" by a choice means you are sure it is the wrong answer. If you were going to guess, you wouldn't guess that answer.

Remember, it is fine to write in your test booklet. Your pencil is a powerful tool! Use it well. Think about Dwight!

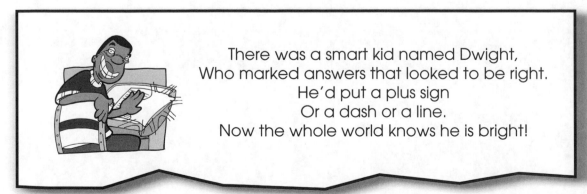

There was a smart kid named Dwight,
Who marked answers that looked to be right.
He'd put a plus sign
Or a dash or a line.
Now the whole world knows he is bright!

Do not get stuck on one question.

One of the biggest mistakes that students make on a state proficiency test is to get stuck on one question. The test gives you many chances to show all that you have learned. If you do not know the answer to one or two questions, your test score will not be ruined. If you spend all of your time worrying and wondering about one or two hard questions, you will not give yourself the chance to answer the questions you do know.

If you feel stuck on a question, make yourself move on. You can come back to this question later and you may be able to answer it then. This is because one question or answer may remind you of how to answer another question that seemed difficult before. Also, when you start answering questions successfully and stop being stuck, you will feel calmer and better about yourself. Then, when you go back to the hard question, you will have the confidence you need to do well. Do not tie up all of your time on one difficult question. No one knows all of the answers on the test. Just circle the question that is giving you trouble and come back to it later. Think about Von!

There was a sweet girl named Von,
Who got stuck and just couldn't go on.
She'd sit there and stare,
But the answer wasn't there.
Before she knew it, all the time was gone.

Use your common sense!

You know a lot more than what you have learned in school. Most people solve problems using what they know from their daily lives as well as many things they have learned in school. When you take the state proficiency test, you should use everything you have learned in school, but you should also use what you have learned outside the classroom to help you answer questions correctly. This is called "using common sense."

Think about a mathematics question that has to do with baking cakes. You are asked to figure out the median temperature at which cakes should be baked. You quickly figure out the answer, and your number shows "3,500° F." Does that seem right to you? If you think about what you know, you know you have never seen 3,500° F on the oven in your house. How could this answer be right? You go back and look at your answer and realize you put a decimal in the wrong place. The correct answer is "350° F." Now you have used your common sense to figure out a correct answer. Although the mathematics question might have been difficult at first, your common sense saved the day. Think about Drew!

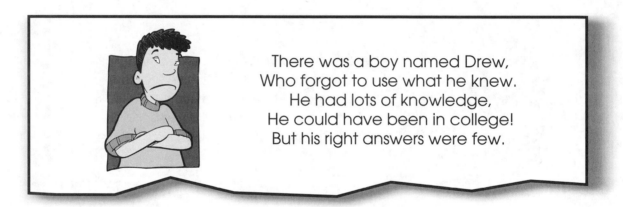

There was a boy named Drew,
Who forgot to use what he knew.
He had lots of knowledge,
He could have been in college!
But his right answers were few.

Always recheck your work.

Everyone makes mistakes. The most mistakes are made when students feel a little worried or rushed. Checking your work is very important. Careless mistakes can easily lead to a wrong answer, even when you have figured out the answer correctly. Always read a paragraph over again if there is something you do not understand. Look to see if there is something you forgot. In the Mathematics section, look at your work to make sure you did not mix one number up with another. Check to make sure your addition, subtraction, multiplication, and division problems are all lined up neatly and are easy to read. If your numbers seem messy, you might have made a mistake. If an answer does not seem to make sense, go back and reread the question or recheck your work. Think about Cath and Jen!

A smart young lady named Cath,
Always forgot to recheck her math.
She thought she was done,
But wrote eleven instead of one!
When her test score comes she won't laugh.

There was a quick girl named Jen,
Who read stuff once and never again.
It would have been nice,
If she read it twice.
Her scores would be better then!

Pay attention to yourself and not to others.

What matters on your state proficiency test is how you do, not how your friends are doing. When you are taking a test, it is easy to look around the room and wonder how your friends are doing. This is a waste of time. Instead, use your time and energy to show what you know.

If you find your attention wandering away from the test, give yourself a little break. Think good thoughts about your state proficiency test and try to put scary thoughts out of your mind. Stretch your arms and feet or move around a little bit in your chair. Anything you can do to pay better attention is a great test-taking strategy. Think about Kirk!

There was a boy named Kirk,
Who thought of everything but his work.
He stared in the air,
And wiggled in his chair.
When his test scores come he won't look!

If you do not understand something, speak up.

No one wants to look dumb. Some students think that if they ask questions about school work or a test, their classmates will think they are dumb. There is nothing wrong with asking questions. Your state proficiency test can be a complicated test. Asking questions about the test will help you do your best. You might be surprised to learn your classmates might have the same questions that you do but are afraid to ask. Don't sit on your hands! Instead, raise them to ask important questions.

Specific Strategies for Online Tests

Kids usually have two different kinds of thoughts about taking a test on a computer. Some say, "Well, I use my computer all the time … I'm not going to even pay attention to the test … computers are easy!" Some kids think in the opposite way. They say, "A computer test? That has to be even scarier than a regular test … there is no way I am going to do well!" The truth is that both of them are wrong. You have to use some special strategies to do your best on computer tests, and when you do, you will do your best!

1. **Read the Directions.** Here is a silly question: Would you want to eat a cake your friend made if he didn't read the directions on the box? Probably not! But even if you aren't a famous cook, you could make a pretty good cake if you read and follow directions. If you read the directions for EACH QUESTION you will have a much better chance of showing what you know. Because even if you know a lot, you have to answer what the question asks. Don't leave out this important step to test success!

2. **Don't Go With the First Answer.** Take a little time and read the WHOLE question and ALL the answer choices. The first answer that looks right is not always the best. Think about going out to dinner with your grandmother. You look at the menu and see "Big Ole Burger"! That sounds good. But if you looked at ALL the menu choices, you might have found your favorite tacos! The burger was good, but if you took more time, you would have found a better choice.

3. **Ask Yourself … How Much Time Do I Have?** You will have a certain amount of time to complete each section of the test. Always check to see how much time you will have. Practice also helps. Did you know that football players practice and practice to see how long it takes to line up and start a play? After a while they are more relaxed and don't worry about time running out. You need to take some practice tests to feel comfortable with timed tests.

4. **Is There a Good Way to Guess?** Most of the time it is a good idea to guess, especially if you can make an "educated" guess! That means you know some things about the question, but not everything. Let's say you aren't quite sure where your cousin lives, but you know it is cold and snows there all the time. One of your friends says that maybe your cousin lives in Georgia. You don't think that is right, because it hardly gets very cold there, and it is right next to Florida! So you can make an educated guess that "Georgia" isn't the right answer!

5. **When Should You Guess?** Unless the directions say that you will lose points for guessing, go for it! Educated guesses are the best, but even if you are really unsure of the answer, calm down and take a guess. If you have four possible answers, and make a guess, you have a one out of four chance of guessing correctly. That is like having three old pennies and one new penny in a bowl. If you just reach in, you will get the new penny one out of every four times you try. That's why you should answer every question!

6. **Don't Mess With That Test Window!** When people get a little nervous, they tend to make silly mistakes. One kid was rushing to make some toast before running off to school, and he unplugged the toaster instead of making the toast! Figure out how the computer screen works, and DON'T close that test window!

7. **Have a Good Attitude!** The better you feel, the better you will do! Remind yourself of how much you have learned in school. Remember that while this test is important, that your teachers will still like you a lot no matter how you do. Just do your best and feel good about yourself. Did you know that when runners have a good attitude, that they win more often? Well, the same goes for you and tests!

8. **If You Have Time Left, Use it!** You can use extra time to help you do your best! If your computer test allows, review your answers, especially if you guessed at a question or two. Take a deep breath and calm down. You might find that a better answer comes into your mind. Talk to yourself a little about some of your answers. You might ask yourself, "I chose the answer that said that it will take 6 hours for that ice cube to melt. That seems like a long time ... maybe I better recheck this and see if that makes sense."

Reading

Introduction

In the Reading section of the *Show What You Know® on the Common Core for Grade 5, Student Workbook*, you will be asked questions to test what you have learned so far in school. These questions are based on the reading skills you have been taught in school through the fifth grade. The questions you will answer are not meant to confuse or trick you but are written so you have the best chance to show what you know.

The *Show What You Know® on the Common Core for Grade 5, Student Workbook* includes two full-length Reading Assessments that will help you practice your test-taking skills.

Glossary

alliteration: Repeating the same sound at the beginning of several words in a phrase or sentence. For example, "The bees buzzed in the back of the blue barn."

adjectives: Words that describe nouns.

adverbs: Words that describe verbs.

antonyms: Words that mean the opposite (e.g., *light* is an antonym of *dark*).

audience: The people who read a written piece or hear the piece being read.

author's purpose: The reason an author writes, such as to entertain, to inform, or to persuade.

author's tone: The attitude the writer takes toward an audience, a subject, or a character. Tone is shown through the writer's choice of words and details. Examples of tone are happy, sad, angry, gentle, etc.

base word (also called root word): The central part of a word that other word parts may be attached to.

biography: A true story about a person's life.

cause: The reason for an action, feeling, or response.

character: A person or an animal in a story, play, or other literary work.

compare: To use examples to show how things are alike.

contrast: To use examples to show how things are different.

details: Many small parts which help to tell a story.

descriptive text: To create a clear picture of a person, place, thing, or idea by using vivid words.

directions: An order or instructions on how to do something or how to act.

draw conclusion: To make a decision or form an opinion after considering the facts from the text.

effect: A result of a cause.

events: Things that happen.

fact: An actual happening or truth.

fiction: A passage that is made up rather than factually true. Examples of fiction are novels and short stories.

format: The way a published piece of writing looks, including the font, legibility, spacing, margins, and white space.

generalize: To come to a broad idea or rule about something after considering particular facts.

genres: Categories of literary and informational works (e.g., biography, mystery, historical fiction, poetry).

graphic organizer: Any illustration, chart, table, diagram, map, etc., used to help interpret information about the text.

heading: A word or group of words at the top or front of a piece of writing.

infer: To make a guess based on facts and observations.

inference: An important idea or conclusion drawn from reasoning rather than directly stated in the text.

inform: To give knowledge; to tell.

informational text (also called expository text): Text with the purpose of telling about details, facts, and information that is true (nonfiction). Informational text is found in textbooks, encyclopedias, biographies, and newspaper articles.

literary devices: Techniques used to convey an author's message or voice (e.g., figurative language, simile, metaphors, etc.).

literary text (also called narrative text): Text that describes actions or events, usually written as fiction. Examples are novels and short stories.

main idea: The main reason the passage was written; every passage has a main idea. Usually you can find the main idea in the topic sentence of the paragraph.

metaphor: A comparison between two unlike things without using the words "like" or "as." An example of a metaphor is, "My bedroom is a junkyard!"

Glossary

mood: The feeling or emotion the reader gets from a piece of writing.

nonfiction: A passage of writing that tells about real people, events, and places without changing any facts. Examples of nonfiction are an autobiography, a biography, an essay, a newspaper article, a magazine article, a personal diary, and a letter.

onomatopoeia: The use of words in which the sound of the word suggests the sound associated with it. For example, buzz, hiss, splat.

opinion: What one thinks about something or somebody; an opinion is not necessarily based on facts. Feelings and experiences usually help a person form an opinion.

passage: A passage or writing that may be fiction (literary/narrative) or nonfiction (informational/expository).

persuade: To cause to do something by using reason or argument; to cause to believe something.

plan: A method of doing something that has been thought out ahead of time.

plot: A series of events that make up a story. Plot tells "what happens" in a story, novel, or narrative poem.

plot sequence: The order of events in a story.

poetry: A type of writing that uses images and patterns to express feelings.

point of view: The way a story is told; it could be in first person, omniscient, or in third person.

predict: The ability of the reader to know or expect that something is going to happen in a text before it does.

prefix: A group of letters added to the beginning of a word. For example, *un*tie, *re*build, *pre*teen.

preposition: A word that links another word or group of words to other parts of the sentence. Examples are in, on, of, at, by, between, outside, etc.

problem: An issue or question in a text that needs to be answered.

published work: The final writing draft shared with the audience.

reliable: Sources used for writing that are trustworthy.

resource: A source of help or support.

rhyme: When words have the same last sound. For example, hat/cat, most/toast, ball/call.

root word (also called base word): The central part of a word that other word parts may be attached to.

schema: The accumulated knowledge that a person can draw from life experiences to help understand concepts, roles, emotions, and events.

sentence: A group of words that express a complete thought. It has a subject and a verb.

sequential order: The arrangement or ordering of information, content, or ideas (e.g., a story told in chronological order describes what happened first, then second, then third, etc.).

setting: The time and place of a story or play. The setting helps to create the mood in a story, such as inside a spooky house or inside a shopping mall during the holidays.

simile: A comparison between two unlike things, using the words "like" or "as." "Her eyes are as big as saucers" is an example of a simile.

solution: An answer to a problem.

stanzas: Lines of poetry grouped together.

story: An account of something that happened.

story elements: The important parts of the story, including characters, setting, plot, problem, and solution.

style: A way of writing that is individual to the writer, such as the writer's choice of words, phrases, and images.

suffix: A group of letters added to the end of a word. For example, teach*er*, color*ful*, sugar*less*, etc.

summary: To retell what happens in a story in a short way by telling the main ideas, not details.

Glossary

supporting details: Statements that often follow the main idea. Supporting details give you more information about the main idea.

symbolism: Something that represents something else. For example, a dove is a symbol for peace.

synonyms: Words with the same, or almost the same, meaning (e.g., sketch is a synonym of draw).

theme: The major idea or topic that the author reveals in a literary work. A theme is usually not stated directly in the work. Instead, the reader has to think about all the details of the work and then make an inference (an educated guess) about what they all mean.

title: A name of a book, film, play, piece of music, or other work of art.

tone: A way of writing that shows a feeling.

topic sentence: A sentence that states the main idea of the paragraph.

valid: Correct, acceptable.

verb: A word that shows action or being.

voice: To express a choice or opinion.

Reading Assessment One

Directions for Taking the Reading Assessment

The Reading Assessment contains six reading selections and 40 questions. Some of the selections are fiction, while others are nonfiction. Read each selection and the questions that follow carefully. You may look back at any selection as many times as you would like. If you are unsure of a question, you can move to the next question, and go back to the question you skipped later.

Multiple-choice questions require you to pick the best answer out of four possible choices. Only one answer is correct. The short-answer questions will ask you to write your answer and explain your thinking using words. Remember to read the questions and the answer choices carefully. You will mark your answers on the answer document.

When you finish, check your answers.

Read this selection. Then answer the questions that follow.

Alligators and Crocodiles

Alligators

1   Alligators are amazing animals. The American alligator lives in the southeast part of the United States, where the weather stays warm. Most grow to be about 10 feet long. Some of the world's biggest alligators have even grown to be 22 feet long!

2   Alligators have broad snouts that are flat and round. An alligator also has a tail, four short legs, skin that is tough and gray, and more than 70 sharp teeth. When the mouth is closed, you cannot see the bottom row of teeth. If a tooth falls out, another grows in to take its place. An alligator can live up to 75 years, and, in its lifetime, it may change teeth over 40 times! Alligators crawl around on land and swish their tails back and forth to move through the water. They cannot control the temperature of their bodies, so, if it gets too cold, they lie in the sun; if it's too hot, they float in the water.

3   Alligators are very sneaky hunters. They will stay in the water and wait for a fish, a frog, or a turtle to come too close and then, SNAP! They will even creep up on animals that have stopped for a quick drink, like birds or raccoons.

4   Like other reptiles, alligators lay their eggs on land. The mother scoops out a hole and lays as many as 50 eggs in it. She then covers the area with mud and plants and stays near the nest. About two months later, when she hears some grunting sounds, she tears the top off the nest and finds her baby alligators blinking up at her.

ALLIGATOR

Go On ▶

Crocodiles

5   Crocodiles live in the tropical and subtropical regions of the world. The American crocodile can be found mostly in Florida. Like all reptiles, crocodiles are coldblooded. This means their body temperatures depend on the environment. To stay warm, a crocodile lies in the sun.

6   The crocodile has a narrow snout. When the mouth is closed, the teeth of the lower jaw are visible. The average crocodile has about 30–40 teeth in its lower jar and has roughly the same number in its upper jaw. The jaws of crocodiles are very powerful and are extremely important for catching food.

7   These reptiles eat fish, frogs, and other small aquatic animals. Some larger crocodiles have been known to feast on deer and oxen. When searching for food, crocodiles submerge themselves in water. The eyes and nose are just above the surface as the reptile waits for a chance to catch its prey.

8   Although she spends much of her time in the water, the female crocodile lays her eggs in sand or mud. The heat of the sun helps the eggs to hatch. Similar to the female alligator, the female crocodile will protect her nest against predators looking to make a meal of her eggs.

CROCODILE

Go On ▶

1. Because crocodiles need to stay warm, most American crocodiles are found –

   A. in muddy places.

   B. in Florida.

   C. near other reptiles.

   D. all over the United States.

2. What is one DIFFERENCE between paragraph 1 of "Alligators" and paragraph 1 of "Crocodiles"?

   A. Paragraph 1 of "Alligators" tells about the length of the reptile, but paragraph 1 of "Crocodiles" does not.

   B. Paragraph 1 of "Alligators" tells about where the reptile lives, but paragraph 1 of "Crocodiles" does not.

   C. Paragraph 1 of "Alligators" does not tell about the length of the reptile, but paragraph 1 of "Crocodiles" does.

   D. Paragraph 1 of "Alligators" does not tell about where the reptile lives, but paragraph 1 of "Crocodiles" does.

Go On ▶

3. Read this sentence from the second paragraph of "Crocodiles."

    "The average crocodile has about 30–40 teeth in its lower jaw and has *roughly* the same number in its upper jaw."

    What does the word *roughly* mean?

    A. painfully

    B. about

    C. difficulty

    D. uneven

5. The author wrote "Alligators" and "Crocodiles"

    A. to entertain the reader with a story about an alligator and a crocodile.

    B. to inform the reader with facts about alligators and crocodiles.

    C. to describe the way alligators and crocodiles hunt.

    D. to explain why alligators and crocodiles can be found in Florida.

4. Which statement tells you about how alligators hunt?

    A. Like other reptiles, alligators lay their eggs on land.

    B. She then covers the area with mud and plants and stays near the nest.

    C. They will even creep up on animals that have stopped for a quick drink, like birds or raccoons.

    D. Alligators crawl around on land and swish their tails back and forth to move through the water.

6. How are crocodiles and alligators ALIKE?

    A. The females do not protect their eggs.

    B. They are both reptiles.

    C. They both have broad snouts.

    D. You can see the bottom row of teeth when the mouth is closed.

Go On ▶

7. Read the chart below.

Alligators	Crocodiles
Bottom teeth are not visible when mouth is closed	Bottom teeth are visible when mouth is closed
Broad snout	**X**
Have more than 70 teeth	Have 30–40 teeth on the top and bottom of their jaws

What should go in Box X?

A. Short snout

B. Small legs

C. Thick skin

D. Narrow snout

8. When does a female alligator know to uncover her nest?

A. when she feels movement underneath the ground

B. when she hears grunting sounds

C. when two months have gone by

D. when the spring comes

Go On

> **Read this selection. Then answer the questions that follow.**

The One, the Only

1　　Think back to the last time you were at a sporting event, like a basketball game. You and your teammates are in the zone, passing the ball to each other while looking for the perfect shot. The ball is passed to you. You set up for the shot and…the play is interrupted by the shrill shriek of the referee's whistle. As you wait for the referee's call, you think to yourself, "That whistle is one of the most annoying noises I've ever heard! The staccato sound that stops the action is horrible!" You continue playing the game, which is frequently interrupted by the noise of the whistle. At the sound of the final whistle, you congratulate the other team and head to the locker room, not giving the whistle any more thought.

2　　Did you know that the only metal whistle factory in the United States is in Ohio? The American Whistle Corporation is located in Columbus, Ohio. The company has been around since 1956, and while there are many competitors throughout the world, the American Whistle Corporation is still the only U.S. manufacturer[1] of metal whistles. The company's motto is: "The one, the only."

3　　Metal whistles make a distinctive fluttering sound when blown. This is caused by the vibration of the pea, or cork ball, that is inserted into the whistles. The pea used to be inserted by hand. Factory workers would pinch the cork balls into the slot at the top of the whistle. Now, a machine has been invented to insert the pea while a factory worker holds the whistle. The balls have just enough give that they can be inserted, but once they are inside the whistle, they can't come out.

4　　An Ohioan designed a machine that is able to create a die to stamp out whistle parts. A die is a form or mold that can be used over and over again to create certain shapes. All of the whistle parts made by the American Whistle Corporation are made from brass because brass carries sound better than other metals. Once the whistle parts have been stamped out, they go through a multi-step process to be formed into whistles. The sections of the whistles are soldered[2] together and the rough edges are rubbed out. Then they go through a bathing process in a stream of water and plastic to help remove any sharp edges or imperfections[3] that may still remain. The cork balls are inserted and rubber safety tips are added. The whistles are then plated in shiny silver or brass.

[1] **manufacturer:** a business that makes a product

[2] **soldered:** when metal pieces are joined together

[3] **imperfections:** a small flaw or defect in a product

Go On

5   One unique thing about the whistles produced in Ohio is that they are the only kind in the world that can have die-struck logos put on them. This is what makes these whistles unique. The American Whistle Corporation makes 24-karat-gold-plated whistles for the referees of the Super Bowl each year. The New York City Police Department orders 10,000 whistles every year. The American Whistle Corporation manufactures about one million whistles a year. That may sound like a lot, but 20 million whistles are made world-wide each year.

6   There are many uses for whistles. Along with sport-related uses, whistles are an effective safety device. Imagine if you were camping in the woods with your family. What would happen if you took a hike in the woods and got lost? How would your parents find you? If you had a whistle, you could blow it until someone came to your aid. Whistles are also used on college campuses throughout the country as part of their safety programs. People can blow on their whistles if they are attacked to scare off the attacker and attract the attention of people who may be nearby. People who go out on boat trips should also carry whistles with them. If their boat won't start, they can blow their whistle to get the attention of other boaters, so that they don't become stranded in the middle of the water.

7   The next time you're at a football game, cheerleading practice, or watching a policeman direct traffic, listen for the whistle that was probably made in Ohio.

Go On ▶

9. Read this sentence from the first paragraph of "The One, The Only."

    "The *staccato* sound that stops the action is horrible!"

    What is the meaning of the word *staccato*, as used in this sentence?

    A. a long, continuous sound

    B. a short, choppy sound

    C. a loud sound

    D. a soft sound

11. Based on the information in the selection, what would happen if metal whistles didn't contain cork balls?

    A. They wouldn't make fluttering noises.

    B. They wouldn't have logos stamped on the side.

    C. They would sound louder.

    D. The whistle sound would fade in and out.

10. Read this sentence from the third paragraph of "The One, The Only."

    "The sections of the whistles are *soldered* together and the rough edges are rubbed out."

    What is the meaning of the word *soldered*, as used in this sentence?

    A. joined

    B. separated

    C. made

    D. erased

Go On ▶

12. Which of the following is not a reason listed as a use for whistles?

   A. safety on a boat

   B. safety while camping

   C. safety on a college campus

   D. safety while making music

13. Read this sentence from the first paragraph of "The One, The Only."

   "You set up for the shot and…the play is interrupted by the *shrill shriek* of the referee's whistle."

   Which of the following is a synonym for the phrase *shrill shriek*?

   A. quiet hum

   B. high-pitched noise

   C. loud booming noise

   D. off-key song

Go On ▶

> **Read this selection. Then answer the questions that follow.**

On the Hunt for a Fossil

1   Have you ever wanted to be a fossilist? Human beings have been searching for fossils for centuries. Fossilists are people who search for fossils. Fossils are the remains of centuries-old plants and animals that have been preserved. Fossils are oftentimes found in sedimentary rock. Sedimentary rock is formed when layers of dirt are compacted together. Examples of sedimentary rock include limestone, sandstone, and shale. Fossils have also been discovered in amber (a yellowish-brown, see-through substance made of hardened sap), ice, and asphalt (a black, tar-like substance now used for paving roads). Some of the oldest fossils are as old as 3.5 billion years. Newer fossils are about 10,000 years old.

2   Paleontologists and fossilists are people who seek out and study fossils and other organic remains. They have gone all over the world looking for these rare relics. Fossils can be found around the globe, from Greenland to Antarctica and everywhere in between. Modern-day paleontologists carry special tools with them, including chipping hammers, chisels, collecting bags, gloves, eye protection, soft brushes, special maps and computers, and small shovels called trowels. They also bring along magnifying glasses so they can see tiny things more clearly. Most also carry notebooks for recording information.

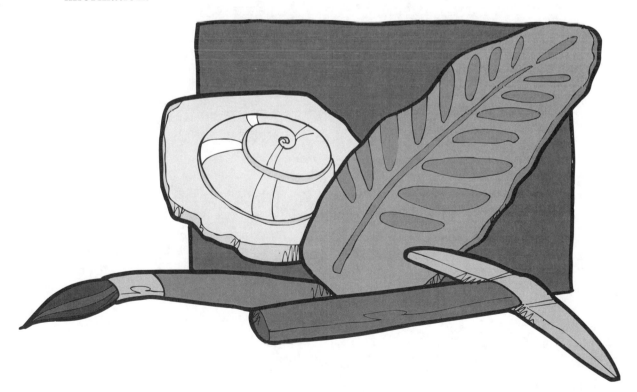

Go On ▶

---

3   Fossilists haven't always had the benefit of maps and special tools, however. Long ago, fossil hunters had to rely on their senses as well as on keen observation. One person known for her early fossil-hunting skills was Mary Anning. She was born in 1799, and her family was very poor, especially after the death of her father in 1810. As a teenager, Mary would often walk the unstable cliffs near her home of Lyme Regis, England, in search of fossils. She collected fossils and sold them to scientists, to collectors, and to museums in order to make money. As her knowledge of fossils and their origins grew, she demonstrated her talents as a well-skilled fossil hunter.

4   Some scientists credit Mary with early discoveries of ichthyosaur and plesiosaurus fossils. Both finds were considered extremely important to the scientific community. Despite her refined talent, Mary had to sell her findings in order to survive. It wasn't until much later in her life that Anning received the recognition she deserved. In 1838, she received wages from the British Association for the Advancement of Science. At around this time, she also received money from the Geological Society of London so she could pay her living expenses. Until her death in 1847, Mary, or "Fossil Woman," as she became known, searched for fossils. During her lifetime, she made important discoveries, including the skeletons of sea serpents and flying dinosaurs.

5   Today, both professionals and beginners enjoy fossil hunting. Although it isn't easy, the search is thrilling. Next time you're out in the back yard, you should take an extra close look at any rocks you find. Maybe you will be the next Mary Anning!

Go On▶

A Modern-Day Fossilist's Checklist

So you want to be a fossilist! Here are a few things every fossilist needs. Having the right tools and the right information is important, especially if you want to bring home more than a few broken stones. Remember to talk with your parents before you decide to do any work as a fossilist. There are many tools you will need their permission to use. After discussing this exciting hobby, maybe you'll get your mom and dad excited about fossils, too.

- ☐ Geologist's Rock Pick: the square end will break up rock, while the pick end will help you dig
- ☐ Chipping Hammer: this hammer has a flat blade that is useful for splitting or trimming rock
- ☐ Chisel: smaller than a chipping hammer, this tool comes in a variety of sizes; it is also good for splitting and trimming smaller rocks
- ☐ Safety Goggles & Gloves: important forms of protection when cutting rock
- ☐ Tweezers: very useful when removing very small pieces
- ☐ Trowel: helpful for digging soft earth
- ☐ Soft Brush: the brush will dust off your search site
- ☐ Compass: will help you find your way
- ☐ Maps: used to identify where you've been and where you're going
- ☐ Measurement Device: you may want to measure the size of your find
- ☐ Magnifying Glass: useful for looking at the smallest details
- ☐ Camera: you may want to take pictures of your find
- ☐ Notebook & Pencil: for taking notes
- ☐ Collecting Bags: plastic bags work just fine; use these to store your fossils
- ☐ Books & Other Resources: field guides will help you identify areas with many fossils; they may also help you identify what you have found; do some research on fossil hunting before you begin–they will discuss techniques for digging, searching, and collecting

Go On ▶

14. List **two** things Mary Anning is credited with discovering.

15. Write a summary of the selection, "On the Hunt for a Fossil."

Include **three** important ideas from the selection in your summary.

16. How are "On the Hunt for a Fossil" and "A Modern-Day Fossilist's Checklist" ALIKE?

A. They both give details about Mary Anning's life.

B. They both define what a fossilist is.

C. They both describe tools used by fossilists hundreds of years ago.

D. They both describe tools used by the fossilist.

17. In paragraph 2, *relics* are –

A. tools used by fossilists.

B. new objects.

C. places on the globe.

D. objects from the past.

Go On ▶

18. What is the main DIFFERENCE between the information in "On the Hunt for a Fossil" and "A Modern-Day Fossilist's Checklist"?

   A. "On the Hunt for a Fossil" highlights information about tools, and "A Modern-Day Fossilist's Checklist" is an informational article.

   B. "On the Hunt for a Fossil" is an informational article, and "A Modern-Day Fossilist's Checklist" highlights information about tools.

   C. "On the Hunt for a Fossil" is a persuasive article, and "A Modern-Day Fossilist's Checklist" highlights information about tools.

   D. "On the Hunt for a Fossil" is an entertaining story about fossil hunting, and "A Modern-Day Fossilist's Checklist" is an informational article about Mary Anning.

19. What was the primary tool used by Mary Anning as she looked for fossils?

   A. a rock pick

   B. a keen sense of observation

   C. a magnifying glass

   D. a computer

Go On

20. Why did Mary Anning first hunt for fossils?

    A. The Geological Society of London paid her to look for fossils.

    B. The British Association for the Advancement of Science wanted her to find fossils.

    C. She sold the fossils she found in order to support her family.

    D. She enjoyed discovering the fossils for her private collection.

21. Which of the following sentences is an opinion?

    A. Having the right tools and the right information is important, especially if you want to bring home more than a few broken stones.

    B. Remember to talk with your parents before you decide to do any work as a fossilist.

    C. There are many tools you will need their permission to use.

    D. Although it isn't easy, the search is thrilling.

Go On

Read this selection. Then answer the questions that follow.

Summer Fun

1 "Wake up!" Meredith shouted at her sleeping brother. "Today is the first day of summer vacation!" Meredith was anxious to start summer fun, but her brother had no interest in anything other than crawling under his soft sheets. Max mumbled something impossible to hear and rolled back over, pulling the comforter over his head.

2 "Mom says we can go to the wave pool if all our chores are done," Meredith said, trying to persuade Max to get out of bed. "Mine are done, so get dressed and get moving. I want to get to the wave pool." She shut his bedroom door and skipped downstairs. Meredith had been up since the crack of dawn. Summer held so many possibilities for fun; she couldn't wait to get started. Her bed was made; her floor was spotless. Her fifth-grade school books had been lined up neatly on the shelf. After finding a spot in her closet for her backpack, all Meredith could think about was summer fun. Her daydream was interrupted by a phone call. Meredith dashed into the kitchen to answer it: "Marshall residence."

3 "Hello. This is Amy. Is Meredith home?"

4 Meredith and Amy had been best friends since first grade and lived in the same neighborhood, just two blocks from each other.

Go On▶

5   "Hi, Amy! Can you believe it's really summer? What do you want to do today?" Meredith asked. "I was thinking about going to the wave pool. Do you want to go with us?" she asked.

6   "Cool. Let me check with my mom." Amy cupped her hand over the phone. "Mommm," she hollered. Even though the phone was covered, Meredith could still hear the voice. "Can I go to the wave pool with Meredith?"

7   Amy knew what the response would be. Her room was a disaster area. Clothes had been thrown on the floor, her backpack and books were spread out on the desk, and CDs were scattered across the bed.

8   She came back to the phone with a response. "I can't go until my room is picked up," Amy said, "and it's a real mess!"

9   "How long do you think you'll be?" Meredith asked.

10   "Well, I think I can get it finished before you leave for the pool," Amy answered, mentally plotting where she could throw all her stuff—under the bed, in her closet, in her drawers, and other favorite hiding spots. "I can sort it all out later," she thought to herself.

11   Meredith knew better; she knew what Amy was planning. Amy was not tidy. She was the messiest person Meredith knew, and if the girls wanted to get to the wave pool, Amy was going to need some help. "Amy, if you don't really clean your room today, you're going to have to face it another day. You'll probably spend most of the summer trying to get your room in order. I'll help you with your room today, and you can help me with some chores later this week. How's that sound?"

12   "Great!" Amy said excitedly. She knew Meredith was right, and she was thankful for some assistance. Amy was nothing like her neat and tidy best friend. In order to have any fun this summer, she needed to silence her mom's groans about a sloppy room. Luckily, Meredith was always there to help.

Go On

22. How can you tell that Amy and Meredith are friends?

Support your answer with **four** details from the passage.

23. Paragraph 12 states that Amy is *thankful* for Meredith's help.

This means Amy —

A. doesn't want anyone to help her.

B. hopes Meredith will help her soon.

C. doesn't think Meredith will be able to help.

D. is glad to have Meredith's help.

24. According to the story, which word best describes Meredith?

A. careless

B. helpful

C. clumsy

D. messy

25. What is the purpose of the word choice used in paragraph 2 to describe Meredith's room?

A. to appeal to a reader's sense of smell

B. to appeal to a reader's sense of taste

C. to appeal to a reader's sense of hearing

D. to appeal to a reader's sense of sight

Go On ▶

26. How is Meredith DIFFERENT from Amy in the story?

   A. Meredith is neat and tidy; Amy is messy.

   B. Meredith enjoys the wave pool; Amy does not.

   C. Meredith is messy; Amy is neat and tidy.

   D. Meredith likes to sleep in.

27. What is the best summary of this story?

   A. Meredith is excited about summer vacation, so she gets up early to do her chores. She invites her friend Amy to go to the wave pool with her, but Amy's mother says Amy can't go until her room is clean. Meredith offers to help her friend clean her room so they can go to the wave pool and have fun.

   B. Meredith is happy that it is summer vacation so she can sleep in. She wants to go the wave pool, but her brother doesn't want to go with her. She calls her friend Amy and the two of them go to the wave pool.

   C. Meredith and her friend Amy both get up early because they are excited about summer vacation. After cleaning their rooms and finishing up their chores, the two friends go to the wave pool to begin their summer fun.

   D. Meredith's friend Amy calls her on the first day of summer vacation and the two friends decide to go to the wave pool. Meredith has to do her chores first, so Amy comes over and the two girls finish Meredith's chores together.

Go On ▶

> **Read this selection. Then answer the questions that follow.**

Toral's Story

1   The sight of the mail truck pulling up to her house every day filled Toral with fear. Each morning at 9:30 a.m., she would kneel next to the front window and wait for the mail to arrive. After the mail truck moved on down the street, Toral would rise slowly and begin the long walk to the mailbox. Even though the mailbox was only across the street, the journey seemed to take forever. Finally, she would reach the shiny black box and pull open the door. Each day for the past five days, the box had held only mail for Toral's parents: bills, catalogs, and junk mail. This day was different, however. There were no catalogs or white envelopes; there was only a single brown envelope that filled up most of the space inside the mailbox. Toral knew it was for her, but she didn't want to remove it. Finally, she reached in and pulled the envelope out far enough to read the label on the front: Toral Johnson.

2   With a sinking heart, Toral took her envelope and headed back to the house. The clouds in the sky were gray to match her mood, and a strong wind blew her hair in swirls around her face. She thought about opening the envelope right there. She could imagine its contents being carried away in the wind. In the end, though, she knew that even losing the information would not save her. Her parents would just get another copy.

3   Toral's pace slowed even more after she entered the house. She finally made her way to the kitchen table, where she peeled open the envelope's seal and dumped its contents on the table. A welcome letter, a daily program, and a list of activities stared up at her. All had the words "Hillsboro Summer Fun Camp" printed at the top. Horseback riding? Swimming? Hiking? None of those activities sounded like fun to her. Toral sighed. There was no longer a way to pretend it might not happen. She was going to summer camp for two long weeks, and she had no choice but to go. She left the paperwork on the counter and headed to the couch to watch TV.

Go On ▶

Samantha's Story

1   Every day, Samantha stared out the front window at 10:00 a.m. That's when the mailman slowly pulled his truck up to the mailbox and dropped off the Perkins' mail. As soon as the white square vehicle headed to the next house, Sam was out the door. She rushed down the brick sidewalk, swung open the white picket fence, and pulled down the mailbox door. She examined the contents as she made her way back to the house. Each day for the past five days, she had found nothing with her name on it. This day was different, however. The inside of the mailbox was crowded. A large, brown envelope took up most of the space inside the metal box. She tugged at the stack of mail, freeing the envelope, her envelope. The label on the front read, "Samantha Perkins."

2   Finally, the information packet from the Hillsboro Summer Fun Camp had arrived. She had been expecting this bundle for a week. Sam couldn't wait to get inside. She wanted to tear into the brown paper right there in the front yard, but it was windy, and she didn't want to lose any of the information.

3   She rushed to the house and made her way to the kitchen. She opened the envelope and carefully laid out its contents on the table. She found a welcome letter, a daily program, and a list of activities, which included horseback riding, swimming, hiking, and arts and crafts. Samantha was a little nervous about going to a place so far away, but, once she saw all the activities, she knew it would be fun. As she looked through each piece, she started to daydream about the two fun-filled weeks of summer camp ahead of her.

Go On

    Copying is Prohibited   © Englefield & Associates, Inc.

28. Based on the information in the story, what conclusion can the reader draw about Toral?

   A. Toral has never been away to summer camp.

   B. Toral does not enjoy outdoor activities.

   C. Toral would like to get a summer job.

   D. Tori is looking forward to summer camp.

29. What do you think would be the **best** part of Samantha's situation?

   What do you think would be the **worst** part of Samantha's situation?

   Include information from the story in your answer.

30. Which of the following sentences lets you know Samantha is excited about summer camp?

   A. "She opened the envelope and carefully laid out its contents on the table."

   B. "As she looked through each piece, she started to daydream about the two fun-filled weeks of summer camp ahead of her."

   C. "She found a welcome letter, a daily program, and a list of activities."

   D. "A large, brown envelope took up most of the space inside the metal box."

31. What words best describe Samantha and Toral?

   A. Samantha is miserable; Toral is happy.

   B. Samantha is clever; Toral is bored.

   C. Samantha is hopeful; Toral is cheerless.

   D. Samantha is calm; Toral is nervous.

Go On ▶

32. What are **two** ways Samantha in "Samantha's Story" and Toral in "Toral's Story" are ALIKE?

What are **two** ways Samantha is DIFFERENT than Toral?

Include information from both stories in your answer.

33. How is the topic of summer camp presented in the two selections, "Samantha's Story" and "Toral's Story"?

A. Both selections talk about summer camp in a negative way.

B. Both selections talk about summer camp in a positive way.

C. Samantha's story talks about summer camp in a positive way; Toral's story talks about summer camp in a negative way.

D. Samantha' s story talks about summer camp in a negative way; Toral's story talks about summer camp in a positive way.

Go On ▶

Read this selection. Then answer the questions that follow.

Texas Horned Lizards

1   The state reptile of Texas is the Texas horned lizard. This unique animal is known for its strange body parts. These lizards look like small dinosaurs with spines on their heads and rows of spines down the sides of their bodies. They also have two long horns, several smaller horns on the center of their heads, and a white stripe down their backs. Another interesting thing about the Texas horned lizard is the markings behind its head. These can be either dark brown spots or yellow and white patches. The lizard itself can be different shades of brown or gray. They are very small animals, with a length of only about 7 inches when full-grown. These lizards have a short tail, a short, pointed nose, and a broad, flattened body.

2   The Texas horned lizard also has many interesting behaviors. This lizard can flatten its body to hide from enemies. This keeps it from casting a shadow and being noticeable. Not only can it flatten its body, but it can also puff up until it looks like a spiky ball. Also, this lizard can hide by changing color slightly to blend into its sandy surroundings. Some species of the horned lizards can also shoot blood from their eyes to ward off enemies. These horned lizards are less active from September to May and are most active in the warmer summer months. They spend most of their time either relaxing in the sun to keep warm, eating, or chasing away enemies. The Texas horned lizard grows up without parents to care for it. The mother will lay about 15 to 40 eggs, but she only guards them and keeps them warm for one day then she leaves the eggs before they hatch.

3   When they eat, the Texas horned lizards flick their tongues and swallow their dinner whole. They also have the ability to puff out and to flatten their bodies to collect rainwater. In order to drink the water they collect, the lizards lower their heads and the water flows along the path created by their scales. These animals eat mostly harvester ants but can also feed on other insects like grasshoppers, beetles, and other small insects.

Go On ▶

---

4   Even though these lizards look fierce, they are at risk. They are hunted by a variety of animals, such as hawks, roadrunners, coyotes, snakes, and even other lizards. This is not their biggest problem. For years many people wanted to keep the horned lizard as a pet, but they are hard to care for as pets and often die from getting poor care. New problems for the lizards happened when fire ants began to spread. Harvester ants that the lizards eat had to move away to escape the fire ants. When humans tried to kill the fire ants using poisons; the poisons also harmed the lizards. The lizards are also at risk because they enjoy living in the open range. These areas are being used to build homes and other buildings. People now live in areas that were once home to only animals like the Texas horned lizard.

5   Predators, loss of food supply, and loss of habitat have caused the population of Texas horned lizards to become smaller. Now, the horned lizards are considered a threatened animal. This means that the law protects the lizards. It is against the law for people to keep these animals as pets, to move them from their homes, or to sell them. Some special groups are also asking the public to collect information about the lizards that live in a certain area. Special places like zoos, show the Texas horned lizard in its natural habitat and provide special care for the reptiles to make sure that the lizards are safe. It is the hope that these groups will be able to teach people about the importance of this interesting reptile, so that they will be able to study and enjoy them for years to come.

Go On

34. Paragraph 4 is mainly about —

   A. the appearance of the horned lizard.

   B. the eating habits of the horned lizard.

   C. how to care for horned lizards.

   D. dangers to the horned lizard.

35. Which word from paragraph 1 helps the reader know what *unique* means?

   A. strange

   B. spines

   C. full-grown

   D. flattened

36. The author of this selection most likely —

   A. wants to protect the lizards.

   B. owns a pet store selling unusual pets.

   C. sells poison to kill fire ants.

   D. builds new homes and shopping malls.

Go On ▶

37. Which sentence from the selection expresses an opinion?

   A. "People now live in areas that were once home to only animals like the Texas horned lizard."

   B. "It is the hope that these groups will be able to teach people about the importance of this interesting reptile, so that they will be able to study and enjoy them for years to come."

   C. "Not only can they flatten their bodies, but they can also puff themselves up until they look like spiky balls."

   D. "Now the horned lizards are considered a threatened animal."

38. Read the web of information from the story.

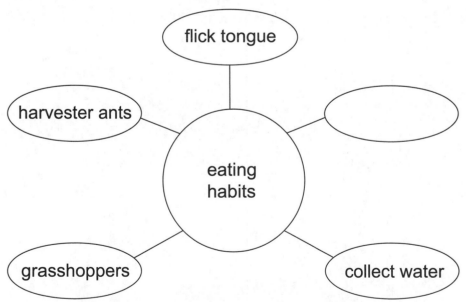

Which of the following belongs in the empty circle of the web?

   A. more active in the summer

   B. changes color

   C. two long horns and several smaller horns

   D. swallow insects whole

Go On

39. How does the author organize paragraphs 4 and 5?

    A. by giving a description of how the lizards use their body parts to eat and hide from enemies

    B. by comparing and contrasting lizards to fire ants

    C. by explaining the problems lizards face and giving the ways humans are helping them

    D. by putting the steps lizards take to hunt in order

40. Why do Texas horned lizards flatten their bodies?

    A. to hide from enemies

    B. to lay eggs

    C. to catch harvester ants

    D. to burrow into the ground

This page intentionally left blank.

1 Ⓐ Ⓑ Ⓒ Ⓓ

2 Ⓐ Ⓑ Ⓒ Ⓓ

3 Ⓐ Ⓑ Ⓒ Ⓓ

4 Ⓐ Ⓑ Ⓒ Ⓓ

5 Ⓐ Ⓑ Ⓒ Ⓓ

6 Ⓐ Ⓑ Ⓒ Ⓓ

7 Ⓐ Ⓑ Ⓒ Ⓓ

8 Ⓐ Ⓑ Ⓒ Ⓓ

9 Ⓐ Ⓑ Ⓒ Ⓓ

10 Ⓐ Ⓑ Ⓒ Ⓓ

11 Ⓐ Ⓑ Ⓒ Ⓓ

12 Ⓐ Ⓑ Ⓒ Ⓓ

13 Ⓐ Ⓑ Ⓒ Ⓓ

14

15

16 Ⓐ Ⓑ Ⓒ Ⓓ

17 Ⓐ Ⓑ Ⓒ Ⓓ

18 Ⓐ Ⓑ Ⓒ Ⓓ

19 Ⓐ Ⓑ Ⓒ Ⓓ

20 Ⓐ Ⓑ Ⓒ Ⓓ

21 Ⓐ Ⓑ Ⓒ Ⓓ

22

23 Ⓐ Ⓑ Ⓒ Ⓓ

24 Ⓐ Ⓑ Ⓒ Ⓓ

25 Ⓐ Ⓑ Ⓒ Ⓓ

26 Ⓐ Ⓑ Ⓒ Ⓓ

27 Ⓐ Ⓑ Ⓒ Ⓓ

28 Ⓐ Ⓑ Ⓒ Ⓓ

29

30 Ⓐ Ⓑ Ⓒ Ⓓ

31 Ⓐ Ⓑ Ⓒ Ⓓ

32

33 Ⓐ Ⓑ Ⓒ Ⓓ

34 Ⓐ Ⓑ Ⓒ Ⓓ

35 Ⓐ Ⓑ Ⓒ Ⓓ

36 Ⓐ Ⓑ Ⓒ Ⓓ

37 Ⓐ Ⓑ Ⓒ Ⓓ

38 Ⓐ Ⓑ Ⓒ Ⓓ

39 Ⓐ Ⓑ Ⓒ Ⓓ

40 Ⓐ Ⓑ Ⓒ Ⓓ

© Englefield & Associates, Inc.

Reading
Assessment Two

Directions for Taking the Reading Assessment

The Reading Assessment contains eight reading selections and 40 questions. Some of the selections are fiction, while others are nonfiction. Read each selection and the questions that follow carefully. You may look back at any selection as many times as you would like. If you are unsure of a question, you can move to the next question, and go back to the question you skipped later.

Multiple-choice questions require you to pick the best answer out of four possible choices. Only one answer is correct. The short-answer questions will ask you to write your answer and explain your thinking using words. Remember to read the questions and the answer choices carefully. You will mark your answers on the answer document.

When you finish, check your answers.

Read this selection. Then answer the questions that follow.

Owen Sunderland
January 22, 2007

Book Report: *The Giver* by Lois Lowry

While I read the novel *The Giver* by Lois Lowry, one question continued to come up in my mind, "What if?"

This story takes place in a community where everyone is the same and no one has feelings, such as pain, joy, sadness, hunger, or love. The people in the community do not make choices either. They are assigned a job in the community at the Ceremony of Twelve when they turn twelve years old.

If a person acts differently from everyone else, then he or she is looked down upon by the community. Everyone in the community is expected to act and be the same. "No one mentioned such things; it was not a rule, but was considered rude to call attention to things that were unsettling or different about individuals," Chapter 3, p. 20.

The main character of *The Giver* is Jonas. During the Ceremony of Twelve, he is assigned the job of Receiver. As Receiver, Jonas must keep all the memories of the community and give wisdom to the Elders of the community so mistakes from the past are not repeated.

Jonas meets with an old, wise man who calls himself the Giver. The Giver gives the community's memories to Jonas by touching Jonas' bare back with his hands. The Giver tells Jonas, "Simply stated, although it's not really simple at all, my job is to transmit to you all the memories I have within me. Memories of the past," Chapter 10, p. 77.

Jonas receives the ability to see color. He feels joy from a thrilling sled ride. He feels warmth and then pain from sitting in the sun and getting a sunburn. And he learns what it feels like to love.

Go On ▶

Jonas realizes that his friends and family will never have feelings or experience life like he does. He is sad that the people whom he loves can never love him back. Jonas wishes he could give memories to other people in the community, but he cannot.

The Giver explains to Jonas that the community decided to make everything the same because they thought it was best for the community. The Giver says, "Our people made that choice, the choice to go to Sameness. Before my time, before the previous time, back and back and back. We relinquished color when we relinquished sunshine and did away with difference. We gained control of many things. But we had to let go of others," Chapter 12, p. 95.

The Giver by Lois Lowry is a novel that will make your imagination soar! It takes you to a place very different from the place we live in today. The novel makes you ask the question "what if?" and makes you realize that a life without feelings – good and bad – is no life at all. I strongly recommend this book to everyone!

Go On ▶

1. According to the selection, which statement is a fact?

   A. Jonas receives the ability to see color.

   B. *The Giver* by Lois Lowry is a novel that will make your imagination soar!

   C. I strongly recommend this book to everyone!

   D. It takes you to a place very different from the place we live in today.

2. Which statement would the author of this book report MOST LIKELY agree with?

   A. Books that spark your imagination are worth reading.

   B. Life would be great if people didn't have feelings.

   C. Books about unlikely stories are not worth reading.

   D. People should only read informational books in class.

Go On ▶

3.   Which excerpt from the selection shows Lois Lowry's description of the Giver's job?

    A. "No one mentioned such things; it was not a rule, but was considered rude to call attention to things that were unsettling or different about individuals," Chapter 3, p. 20.

    B. The Giver gives the community's memories to Jonas by touching Jonas' bare back with his hands.

    C. "Simply stated, although it's not really simple at all, my job is to transmit to you all the memories I have within me. Memories of the past," Chapter 10, p. 77.

    D. The Giver explains to Jonas that the community decided to make everything the same because they thought it was best for the community.

Go On

Read this selection. Then answer the questions that follow.

Soccer

1   Soccer is a popular sport played worldwide both professionally and for fun. In over 200 countries, soccer is played by people of all ages. Only in the United States is the game referred to as "soccer." In other parts of the world, it is referred to as "football" or "futbol."

2   Historians have found evidence that suggests that ancient people made up and participated in different kicking games similar to soccer. The game of soccer as we know it today began in England around the 19th century. Official rules were written for games involving ball handling in the late 1800s, and, at that time, the game allowed for greater use of the hands than is permitted with modern soccer. A meeting of the London Football Association in 1863, however, split football into two sports. The first was rugby football, which is the parent sport of American football. This game allowed for touching and carrying the ball. The second sport was association football, or soccer, which did not allow the use of the hands.

3   Throughout the rest of the 1800s, soccer's popularity was widespread in England and Scotland. British traders, sailors, and soldiers carried the sport to Germany, Italy, Austria, and South America. In 1904, the Federation Internationale de Football Association (FIFA) was formed. FIFA is still the worldwide governing body of soccer. In 1930, FIFA organized the first World Cup, soccer's premier tournament that is held every four years.

4   Soccer was not always such a popular sport in America. While many other countries throughout Europe and South America embraced the game of soccer, people in the United States were slow to accept the sport. It wasn't until the 1970s that the North American Soccer League gained the interest of fans in the United States. Although the league eventually went out of business because of financial problems, it left a lasting impression on Americans, particularly among young people. Today, soccer is the fastest-growing high school and college sport in the United States.

Go On ▶

4. Before football was split into two sports in 1863, —

A. people played kicking games similar to soccer.

B. people in the United States became more interested in soccer.

C. the game of rugby football was created.

D. the first World Cup was organized by FIFA.

6. Look at the dictionary entry for the word *accept*.

> **ac•cept** \ak sept´\ *verb*
> 1. To admit to a group
> 2. To receive gladly and with interest 3. To answer "yes" to an invitation
> 4. To agree to pay

Which definition best matches the meaning of the word *accept* in paragraph 4 of the selection?

A. Definition 1

B. Definition 2

C. Definition 3

D. Definition 4

5. How does the author organize this selection?

A. by giving the history of soccer in time order

B. by comparing and contrasting two types of soccer

C. by describing the game of soccer

D. by listing the problems of the North American Soccer League, then giving solutions

7. The author probably wrote this selection to —

A. explain the rules of soccer.

B. entertain readers with funny stories about soccer.

C. inform readers about the history of soccer.

D. persuade readers to join a soccer team.

Go On ▶

8. Look at the web about soccer from the selection.

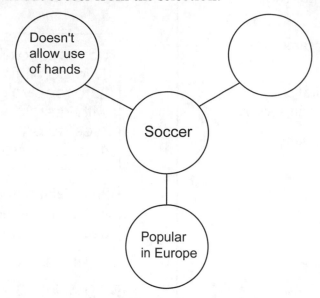

Which of the following belongs in the empty circle of the web?

A. Allows for young players only

B. Allows for carrying the ball

C. Also called rugby football

D. Also called association football

9. In your own words, summarize the selection "Soccer."

Support your answer with **two** details about the sport.

Go On ▶

10. Which sentence from the selection shows why soccer is such a fast-growing high school and college sport in the United States?

    A. "While many other countries throughout Europe and South America embraced the game of soccer, people in the United States were slow to accept the sport."

    B. "Although the league eventually went out of business because of financial problems, it left a lasting impression on Americans, particularly among young people."

    C. "Historians have found evidence that suggests ancient people made up and participated in different kicking games similar to soccer."

    D. "In 1930, FIFA organized the first World Cup, soccer's premier tournament that is held every four years."

Go On

> **Read this selection. Then answer the questions that follow.**

Could Not Wait

1   Sneaking through the mansion's gate,
    my exploration could not wait.

2   From room to room, I gazed high, then low,
    what I would find, I did not know.

3   The rooms were stark[1], the fixtures dark,
    and I was all alone.

4   But not for long,
    Something's wrong: the visitors are two;
    if I'm caught–though I'd rather not–surely I'll be through!

5   In these few words he said to me,
    "I wonder if you'll look at me."

6   I stopped and stared and did not know
    the voice from a face that did not show.

7   I walked four steps and turned around;
    there were no footsteps on the ground.

8   I slinked and crouched all through the hall,
    but the voice shouted out: boy, stand up tall!

9   Scared, I knew not what to do–
    house, I thought, I'm through with you.

10   Quickly, I zipped passed a mirror,
    when suddenly there was a cheer.

11   "You looked, you looked, you looked at me,"
    the tall, framed mirror shouted out with glee.

[1] stark: bare

Go On ▶

12   Haunted by the ghostly shout,
        I rushed to find my exit out.

13   "Oh no, oh no, please, please don't go.
        I promise I am not your foe."

14   Down the hall, and down the stairs,
        I wonder why this mirror cares.

15   No time for that, don't want to chat.
        I'll be gone in seconds flat.

16   I made it through the mansion's gate,
        to get away, I could not wait.

Go On ▶

11. The author wrote this poem

   A. to describe a boy's experience
      inside an empty mansion.

   B. to inform the reader about
      famous haunted mansions.

   C. to persuade the reader to avoid
      empty mansions.

   D. to explain how to be safe inside
      an empty mansion.

13. Which words best describe the inside
    of the mansion?

   A. bright; well-decorated

   B. ugly; small

   C. unlit; empty

   D. cheery; sunny

14. What is the MAIN idea of the poem?

   Support your answer with **two** details
   from the poem.

12. How does the narrator know he is
    not alone in the mansion?

   A. He hears footsteps.

   B. He hears a voice.

   C. Someone grabs his arm.

   D. He sees someone.

Go On

15. What problem does the narrator of this poem face?

    A. The narrator gets caught sneaking in an old mansion.

    B. The narrator is lost in an old mansion.

    C. The narrator is scared by a mirror that talks to him.

    D. The narrator doesn't have a place to live.

16. Which of the following events happened first?

    A. The mirror says, "I wonder if you'll look at me."

    B. The mirror cheers when the boy looks at it.

    C. The boy slinks and crouches through the hall.

    D. The mirror tells the boy not to leave.

Go On

Read this selection. Then answer the questions that follow.

New Kid in Town

1   Tony felt like the shortest boy in class, and, to make matters worse, he was the new kid on the block! Making friends wasn't the easiest thing to do in a new school. His mother told him he would fit right in with the other children, but, for some reason, he just wasn't sure.

2   During homeroom, a brown-haired boy wearing a gray T-shirt said "Hi" to Tony, but none of the other kids seemed to notice him. When the teacher called out his last name, she mispronounced it, and everyone laughed. Tony lowered his head and stared at the top of his desk. He didn't want to see the kids laughing at him; the sound of their laughter was bad enough. The teacher began her morning lesson. Tony couldn't focus. "This day couldn't move any slower," he thought to himself. Time slowly crept by. Every so often, Tony would peek up at the clock. He was careful not to let his eyes move off the desk for very long.

3   Tony wasn't sure of the new school's schedule, so the ringing lunch bell surprised him. The new student walked down the hall to his locker and put his books away. In the cafeteria, he went through the line and got his tray. He found a table near the window and sat alone. The air around him felt cold, unlike his old school, which always felt warm and inviting. "If only I could go back to my old school," he wished to himself as he ate another bite of pizza. "I'd have all of my old friends, and everything would be back to normal," he thought.

4   Changing schools had been hard for Tony. His father had taken a new job halfway through the school year. Tony had to say goodbye to his friends, to his teachers, and to the only home he had ever known. Tony didn't want to finish his lunch. He knew as soon as he did, he would have to make his way to the playground. He would watch all the other kids have fun as he stood off to the side. "I wonder if I can sit here until it's time to go back to class," he thought.

5   Tony gazed out the window. A group of boys from homeroom was playing kickball on the playground. The lunch monitor strolled past Tony and gave him a look that suggested he had better move along soon. He finished his milk and got up to put away his trash. Tony put on his coat, shoved his hands deep into his pockets, and headed out to watch the crowd. He sought out a place by the fence and slumped down to sit on the ground. He kept his head buried.

Go On ▶

---

6   "Hey! Hey you!" At first Tony didn't realize the voice was calling out for him. "You're the new kid, aren't you?" the boy in the gray T-shirt shouted.

7   "Yeah, I'm Tony." He lifted his eyes and squinted as the sunlight hit his face. He was afraid the boy would make fun of him by mispronouncing his last name the way his teacher had.

8   The boy ran to where Tony was sitting. "I'm Solomon, but everyone just calls me Solo. I'm going to play kickball with the other guys. We need another player to make the teams even. Do you know how to play kickball?"

9   "Yeah, sure," he replied.

10   "Great!" Solo said. Solo reached out his hand and pulled Tony to his feet. Tony realized he wasn't the shortest kid in class. He and Solo stood eye to eye. The boys ran toward the makeshift field. "Tony's gonna play," Solo yelled. Tony was worried someone would object, but the only words anyone uttered were, "Next up!"

11   Tony took his seat with his team. The boys started quizzing him on his old school and where he used to live. Everyone was interested in what he had to say, and he appreciated the attention. The kickball game ended with a winning run scored by Tony's team. As the boys celebrated, Tony realized being a new kid in town wasn't so bad after all.

Go On

17. What do you think the theme of this story is? Why?

Explain your answer.

18. What problem does Tony face in the story?

A. He thinks his parents don't care about him.

B. He is afraid he won't be good at kickball.

C. He is worried he won't be able to make friends at his new school.

D. He doesn't think the kids in his new neighborhood will like him.

19. What would Tony most likely do if another new kid came to the class?

A. Tony would invite the new kid to play kickball on the playground.

B. Tony would laugh at the new kid in the cafeteria.

C. Tony would mispronounce the new kid's name to make fun of him.

D. Tony would tell the new kid not to make friends with Solomon.

20. In paragraph 2, the word *mispronounced* means —

A. spelled the wrong way

B. said the wrong way

C. said the correct way

D. spelled the correct way

Go On ▶

21. Why is it important for the reader to know this story takes place in the middle of the school year rather than at the beginning of the school year?

 A. At the beginning of the school year, the teacher would not mispronounce Tony's name.

 B. At the beginning of the school year, none of the students would play kickball.

 C. At the beginning of the school year, Tony's father would not have to get a new job.

 D. At the beginning of the school year, there might be other new students in Tony's class.

23. In paragraph 2, Tony stares at his desk because —

 A. he can't read the board.

 B. he doesn't want to look at the kids who are laughing at him.

 C. he doesn't want to look out the window and see kids playing kickball.

 D. he wants to read a book instead of listening to the teacher's lesson.

22. What conclusion can be made about Tony?

 A. He is the shortest kid in class.

 B. He is happy to be at the new school.

 C. He is the same height as Solomon.

 D. He doesn't like to play kickball.

Go On

> **Read this selection. Then answer the questions that follow.**

First Women of NASA

1   The National Aeronautics and Space Administration (NASA) was created by President Dwight D. Eisenhower in 1958. Many important events have happened since then. On July 20, 1969, Neil Armstrong and Buzz Aldrin walked on the moon. The first space shuttle was launched in 1981, and since that time there have been 112 successful flights. In 2000, the United States and Russia sent people to work on the international space station that was developed by sixteen different nations. Some of those important moments have included the women of NASA. Two special women have become famous for leading the way as American astronauts.

2   Sallie Kirsten Ride was born in Encino, California, on May 26, 1951. Dr. Ride's interesting journey began in 1973 when she finished studying at Stanford University and earned a degree in English and Physics. She continued her education in astrophysics, the study of objects and planets in space. In 1978, she began training with NASA. She completed her NASA training in 1979. Dr. Ride was chosen as an astronaut and became the first American woman in space at the age of 32.

3   Her first mission was aboard the shuttle Challenger, which was launched on June 18, 1983. The trip lasted for six days. During this time she worked with her fellow astronauts to conduct a variety of science experiments. As an astronaut, Sallie Ride became known for her ability to work as a team player and to solve difficult problems. Dr. Ride's second and final trip into space was in October 1984. During her career as an astronaut, she logged a total of almost 200 hours in space.

4   Dr. Ride retired from her work as an astronaut in 1987, but she continued to work on special projects at NASA. For instance, she began the EarthKAM project, which allowed middle school students to take pictures of Earth from space. She also helped NASA to study the two terrible space shuttle accidents: Challenger in 1986 and Columbia in 2003.

5   Another former astronaut, Kathryn Sullivan, was born on October 3, 1951. She earned a degree in Earth Sciences from the University of California, Santa Cruz. During this time, she earned a degree in Geology, the study of rocks and minerals that make up Earth and other planets. Before becoming an astronaut, Dr. Sullivan worked as a scientist who studied the ocean for the United States Geological Survey. Like Sallie Ride, Dr. Sullivan was chosen to work in NASA's space program in 1978 and became an astronaut in 1979.

Go On ▶

6　　　Kathryn Sullivan's first trip to space began on October 5, 1984, with a crew of seven members, including her friend Sallie Ride. During this trip, Dr. Sullivan made history when she became the first American woman to walk in space. This team studied Earth from outerspace and learned how to work with equipment that was sent into space.

7　　　Dr. Sullivan spent over 530 hours in space and completed a total of three trips to space. In April of 1990, she was a member of the crew of the space shuttle Discovery that set up the Hubble Space Telescope. Her last space mission launched on March 24, 1992, and lasted over 8 days. This was the first trip to space dedicated to learning more about the climate of Earth.

8　　　These two women, along with a many other excellent astronauts and scientists, have helped the United States to secure its place as a leader in exploring space and in creating and using space equipment. Today, almost 50 years after it began, NASA continues its mission to explore our universe by creating new equipment for space flight and working in space. Although Sallie Ride and Kathryn Sullivan no longer work at NASA, they continue their work in science by encouraging young people to study science and to become scientists.

24. Which of the following is the best summary of the selection?

    A. Kathryn Sullivan was the first American woman to walk in space. She went to space three times. Dr. Sullivan helped to set up the Hubble Space Telescope. She has had many different jobs as a scientist, but she will always be remembered for her work at NASA.

    B. Sallie Ride was born in California and studied science in school. She became the first American woman astronaut and was very good at solving problems. She no longer works for NASA, but she is still a scientist.

    C. NASA has had many important moments that included female astronauts. For example, Sallie Ride was the first American woman in space, and she was famous for solving problems. Kathryn Sullivan became the first American woman to walk in space. These women still work as scientists and encourage children to study science.

    D. NASA is made up of a group of scientists who study and work in space. Astronauts are important to NASA's work, and so is the equipment that the astronauts use. The Hubble Space Telescope is one of the most important pieces of equipment used by NASA because it has helped NASA to collect information about the different planets in space.

25. What does the word *retired* mean in paragraph 4?

    A. stopped working

    B. took pictures

    C. solved problems

    D. conducted experiments

Go On

26. In paragraph 1, the word *successful* means —

    A. frightful.

    B. sad.

    C. difficult.

    D. able to do well.

27. How does the author organize this selection?

    A. The author lists the steps the reader can take to become an astronaut.

    B. The author describes the inside of a space shuttle.

    C. The author tells a story about a girl named Sallic who works on the space station.

    D. The author explains the ways women have been an important part of the space program in the United States.

28. Why was Sallie Ride chosen to help study the space shuttle accidents?

    A. She was the first American woman in space.

    B. She is good at solving difficult problems.

    C. She took three trips to space.

    D. She helped to set up the Hubble Space Telescope.

Go On ▶

Read this selection. Then answer the questions that follow.

School Uniforms

1   Dear Editor,

2   We have to wear uniforms to school every day because the school board
and many parents think it's better for us. Our uniforms are boring. We wear
polo shirts or button-down shirts, which have to be light blue or white, and
brown shoes. The boys wear khaki pants, and the girls wear khaki skirts.

3   I've talked with many of my friends, and we think uniforms are bad for
our mental health. Putting on the same outfit every day is really depressing.
We don't want to go to school depressed. It's hard to get our work done, and
all our creativity is drained.

4   According to my teacher, the uniforms remind us that we are all equal.
While I don't disagree that we are all equal, I think people send this message,
not clothes. The uniform covers up each student's uniqueness. Even though
we are all equal, we are all distinct. There are differences in our school, and
I think we should be allowed to wear clothes we have picked out in order
to express our unique qualities. Haven't we always been told that it doesn't
matter what's on the outside; it's what's inside that counts?

5   If teachers think uniforms are such a great idea, why don't they wear
them? Lakewood teachers are allowed to express themselves with an
individual sense of style. If the teachers had to wear the same outfit each day,
I know they would feel differently about the uniform rule.

6   Uniforms are bad for our mental health. The uniforms tell us we have to
look the same to be equal and we shouldn't express who we are. We should be
allowed to make our own decisions about what to wear every day.

7   Sincerely,

8   Amber Gianetti, Lakewood Elementary School

Go On

29. Describe the Lakewood Elementary School uniforms.

    Give **two** details of what the uniforms look like.

30. What makes Amber's arguments believable?

    A. She researched the effects of school uniforms on students' mental health at the library.

    B. She found a student online who felt the same way she did about wearing school uniforms.

    C. She knows how it feels to wear a uniform every day; she's speaking from experience.

    D. She is a teacher, so she is very smart and knows many things.

31. All of the author's problems with the uniforms are connected by the idea that –

    A. students have to wear uniforms, but teachers don't.

    B. students have to wear the same clothes every day, and all students look the same.

    C. the colors in the uniforms are boring, and they make students depressed.

    D. the boys are allowed to wear polo shirts, but the girls are not.

Go On ▶

Read this selection. Then answer the questions that follow.

Hummingbirds

1   Have you ever heard the humming sound of the hummingbird? These tiny birds get their name from the sound they make when their wings beat rapidly in the air. The wingbeat rate of hummingbirds depends on the size of the bird. The largest hummingbird, the Giant Hummingbird, has a wingbeat rate of 10 to 15 beats per second. The smallest hummingbird has a wingbeat of more than 80 per second. Your chances of catching a long gaze of a hummingbird are not good, however. Hummingbirds don't hang around in one spot for very long.

2   Hummingbirds are active during the day. They feed on nectar. Nectar is a sweet substance found in flowers. You might see these flowers in your garden or in the back yard. You can also put up a feeder and fill it with sugar water to attract hummingbirds to your house. Hummingbirds are attracted to bright red- and orange-colored blooms more than to other colors. To get to the nectar, hummingbirds reach their lengthy tongues down into the flowers. Nectar isn't the only thing that the hummingbird likes to eat. It will also eat tiny insects that hide out in the flowers. Hummingbirds are not specifically hunted by other animals. However, animals that have been known to eat hummingbirds include cats, small hawks, owls, and seagulls.

3   One unusual feature of the hummingbird is that it can fly backwards. This comes in handy when the bird flies toward and away from flowers as it gathers nectar. It is the only bird with this unique gift.

4   There are about two dozen types of hummingbirds in the United States. The ruby throated hummingbird is the most common. It can be found throughout the South. It is about four inches long and is easy to spot. Male ruby throats are shiny green in color. They have brilliant red throats and white breasts. The female is less brightly colored. It does not have a ruby throat. The iridescent colors of hummingbird plumage are caused by a combination of the refraction of light off of some of their feathers and pigmentation. Hummingbirds have an average lifespan of 3 to 4 years, although there is a record of one bird living for 12 years.

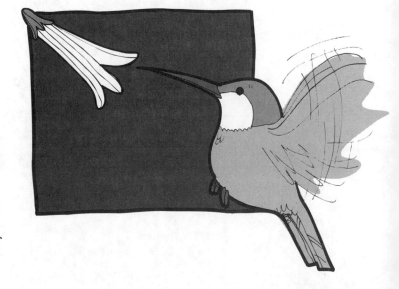

Go On

32. According to the information in the selection, what causes the iridescent color of hummingbird plumage?

   A. light refraction off their feathers only

   B. pigmentation of the hummingbird only

   C. a combination of light refraction and hummingbird pigmentation

   D. rapid beating of hummingbird wings

34. How did hummingbirds get their name?

   A. from the sound made when their wings beat rapidly in the air

   B. from the sound made when they feed on nectar

   C. from the sound made when they fly backward

   D. from the sound made when their feathers refract light

33. Which sentence explains why hummingbirds have shiny colors?

   A. "Male ruby throats are shiny green in color."

   B. "They have brilliant red throats and white breasts."

   C. "The iridescent colors of hummingbird plumage are caused by a combination of the refraction of light off of some of their feathers and pigmentation."

   D. The female is less brightly colored.

Go On ▶

Read this selection. Then answer the questions that follow.

The Gift

1   Ming looked at the stacks of books. As she walked up and down each aisle, she quickly became confused. The dark wood shelves were as tall as the trees in her yard. Each row led to another row, which led to more stacks that contained even more brightly colored books. "What have I gotten myself into?" she thought to herself. Time ticked by, and, just when it seemed as though Ming would never find another human being in the maze of books, she stumbled upon a sales clerk.

2   The clerk's bright yellow T-shirt read, "Let Me Help You." Ming couldn't have been more pleased. "Just in time," she thought to herself. "I was about to give up on this place." Mother's Day was just around the corner, and Ming was on the hunt for the perfect gift. There was just one problem: Ming had no idea what type of book she wanted to buy.

3   The lady in the yellow shirt had an idea. "When you were a little girl, did your mom like to read you stories?" Ming nodded. "You should pick out your favorite storybook. It will remind the two of you of your special memories, and you can write a special thank-you note on the inside cover. Your mom will love it!" The clerk spoke so quickly that Ming didn't have time to object.

Go On▶

---

4   The clerk was very enthusiastic as she marched Ming toward the children's book corner. The white stacks were the perfect height. Ming could even reach the top rows. The book titles were familiar, and the carpet beneath her feet featured white clouds in a blue sky.

5   The clerk sat patiently in a rocking chair, and Ming looked over the shelves. Some of the books she had seen before; others seemed brand new. Ming carefully studied the titles, but it wasn't until she reached the very bottom row that she found a copy of The Magic of Myra Brown. "This is it," she thought. The cover featured a freckle-faced redhead who wore a crooked witch's hat. A small black cat peered around Myra's leg, and the title stood out in bold red letters. "I'll take this one," she said to the clerk.

6   Ming pulled a wad of crumpled money from her jacket pocket. The clerk rang up the book, then found a special pen for Ming's inscription. Ming thought for a moment before writing, "Mom: Thank you for always making me feel as magical as Myra. Love, Ming."

7   "Perfect," said the clerk.

8   "Thank you so much," Ming replied. She held the book tightly as she made her way out the door. Ming was proud of the special gift. She couldn't wait for Mother's Day to arrive.

Go On

Emaline's Father's Day Search

1   Hi everyone. My name is Emaline, but you can call me Emma. Today, I am going to tell the story of the hardest thing I've had to do this year. It wasn't a test or a school project; the hardest thing I've done this year is search for a Father's Day present. I learned a lot from my search, and I want to pass along some advice to keep you from making the same mistake I made.

2   I guess maybe I shouldn't have procrastinated[1], but I was too busy to find time to go shopping. So, on the day before Father's Day, I started my search. Of course, when I started, I didn't realize it was going to be a search. I thought the perfect gift would simply jump out at me, and I would be on my way home.

3   When I got to the mall, it was already filled with shoppers. I couldn't believe how many people were there! I took a deep breath and started to move with the crowd. I had a list of stores in my mind, and I was sure the perfect gift would be waiting at one of them. However, at each of the stores, I was greeted with the same situation: the special "Father's Day" section that had been set up was nearly empty. All that was left anywhere were silly little joke gifts, and none of these even came close to being the perfect gift I was hoping to find.

4   After hours of searching, I started my walk home empty-handed. I had failed in my search to find the perfect gift. Instead, my dad was going to be getting yet another card made from construction paper for Father's Day. I knew he wouldn't mind, but I sure did. I shouldn't have waited until the last minute to start shopping. I should have had an idea in mind when I set out. These two things, I've decided, are the most important things to remember when you are buying a gift, so I want to pass them along as tips for gift-buying success.

5   So to all the kids out there, this message is for you! Don't put things off the way I did. If you're looking for the perfect gift, you have to do some planning first. Plan ahead and get started early, and hopefully your search will have a happier ending than mine did.

[1] **procrastinated:** to put off intentionally and habitually

Go On

35. Based on Emma's actions in the selection, which of the following would be the most likely to happen?

   A. Emma does all her chores before she is asked.

   B. Emma turns in homework assignments before they are due.

   C. Emma is always the first person to finish school projects.

   D. Emma waits until the last minute to start school projects.

36. If Emma had found the perfect gift on her search, how would her attitude most likely be different?

   A. Emma wouldn't think shopping at the mall was a good idea.

   B. Emma wouldn't think so many shoppers should be at the mall.

   C. Emma wouldn't think waiting until the last minute was such a bad idea.

   D. Emma wouldn't think anyone should try to find the perfect gift.

37. What is different about the two girls at the end of each selection?

   A. Ming is unhappy with her find; Emma is proud of the result of her search.

   B. Ming is proud of her find; Emma is unhappy with the result of her search.

   C. Ming doesn't think she has found the perfect gift; Emma thinks the gift she has found is perfect.

   D. Ming finds her perfect gift at the bookstore; Emma finds her perfect gift at the mall.

Go On

38. For her best friend's birthday, Ming would probably —

   A. forget to buy a gift.

   B. spend time searching for the perfect gift.

   C. buy a gift her friend wouldn't like.

   D. make someone else choose the gift.

39. What is SIMILAR about these two selections?

   A. Both are about someone who is having trouble finding the perfect gift.

   B. Both are about someone who is shopping in a bookstore.

   C. Both are about someone who is looking for a Father's Day gift at the mall.

   D. Both are about someone who waits too long to start shopping.

40. Read the sentence from the story.

"Time ticked by, and, just when it seemed as though Ming would never find another human being in the maze of books, she *stumbled upon* a sales clerk."

What does the phrase *stumbled upon* mean as used in the sentence?

   A. fell onto a sales clerk

   B. finally found a sales clerk

   C. tripped over a sales clerk

   D. ran into a sales clerk

1 Ⓐ Ⓑ Ⓒ Ⓓ

2 Ⓐ Ⓑ Ⓒ Ⓓ

3 Ⓐ Ⓑ Ⓒ Ⓓ

4 Ⓐ Ⓑ Ⓒ Ⓓ

5 Ⓐ Ⓑ Ⓒ Ⓓ

6 Ⓐ Ⓑ Ⓒ Ⓓ

7 Ⓐ Ⓑ Ⓒ Ⓓ

8 Ⓐ Ⓑ Ⓒ Ⓓ

9

10 Ⓐ Ⓑ Ⓒ Ⓓ

11 Ⓐ Ⓑ Ⓒ Ⓓ

12 Ⓐ Ⓑ Ⓒ Ⓓ

13 Ⓐ Ⓑ Ⓒ Ⓓ

14

15 Ⓐ Ⓑ Ⓒ Ⓓ

16 Ⓐ Ⓑ Ⓒ Ⓓ

17

© Englefield & Associates, Inc.

18 Ⓐ Ⓑ Ⓒ Ⓓ

19 Ⓐ Ⓑ Ⓒ Ⓓ

20 Ⓐ Ⓑ Ⓒ Ⓓ

21 Ⓐ Ⓑ Ⓒ Ⓓ

22 Ⓐ Ⓑ Ⓒ Ⓓ

23 Ⓐ Ⓑ Ⓒ Ⓓ

24 Ⓐ Ⓑ Ⓒ Ⓓ

25 Ⓐ Ⓑ Ⓒ Ⓓ

26 Ⓐ Ⓑ Ⓒ Ⓓ

27 Ⓐ Ⓑ Ⓒ Ⓓ

28 Ⓐ Ⓑ Ⓒ Ⓓ

29

30 Ⓐ Ⓑ Ⓒ Ⓓ

31 Ⓐ Ⓑ Ⓒ Ⓓ

32 Ⓐ Ⓑ Ⓒ Ⓓ

33 Ⓐ Ⓑ Ⓒ Ⓓ

34 Ⓐ Ⓑ Ⓒ Ⓓ

35 Ⓐ Ⓑ Ⓒ Ⓓ

36 Ⓐ Ⓑ Ⓒ Ⓓ

37 Ⓐ Ⓑ Ⓒ Ⓓ

38 Ⓐ Ⓑ Ⓒ Ⓓ

39 Ⓐ Ⓑ Ⓒ Ⓓ

40 Ⓐ Ⓑ Ⓒ Ⓓ

Mathematics

Introduction

In the Mathematics section of the *Show What You Know® on the Common Core for Grade 5, Student Workbook*, you will be asked questions to test what you have learned so far in school. These questions are based on the mathematics skills you have been taught in school through the fifth grade. The questions you will answer are not meant to confuse or trick you but are written so you have the best chance to show what you know.

The *Show What You Know® on the Common Core for Grade 5, Student Workbook,* includes two full-length Mathematics Assessments that will help you practice your test-taking skills.

Copying is Prohibited

Glossary

addend: Numbers added together to give a sum. For example, 2 + 7 = 9. The numbers 2 and 7 are addends.

addition: An operation joining two or more sets where the result is the whole.

a.m.: The hours from midnight to noon; from Latin words *ante meridiem* meaning "before noon."

analyze: To break down information into parts so that it may be more easily understood.

angle: A figure formed by two rays that meet at the same end point called a vertex. Angles can be obtuse, acute, right, or straight.

area: The number of square units needed to cover a region. The most common abbreviation for area is *A*.

Associative Property of Addition: The grouping of addends can be changed and the sum will be the same.
Example: (3 + 1) + 2 = 6; 3 + (1 + 2) = 6.

Associative Property of Multiplication: The grouping of factors can be changed and the product will be the same.
Example: (3 x 2) x 4 = 24; 3 x (2 x 4) = 24.

attribute: A characteristic or distinctive feature.

average: A number found by adding two or more quantities together and then dividing the sum by the number of quantities. For example, in the set {9, 5, 4}, the average is 6: 9 + 5 + 4 = 18; 18 ÷ 3 = 6. *See mean.*

axes: Plural of axis. Perpendicular lines used as reference lines in a coordinate system or graph; traditionally, the horizontal axis (*x*-axis) represents the independent variable and the vertical axis (*y*-axis) represents the dependent variable.

bar graph: A graph using bars to show data.

capacity: The amount an object holds when filled.

chart: A way to show information, such as in a graph or table.

circle: A closed, curved line made up of points that are all the same distance from a point inside called the center.
Example: A circle with center point *P* is shown below.

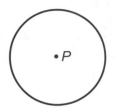

circle graph: Sometimes called a pie chart; a way of representing data that shows the fractional part or percentage of an overall set as an appropriately-sized wedge of a circle.
Example:

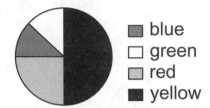

- ■ blue
- □ green
- ▨ red
- ■ yellow

circumference: The boundary line or perimeter of a circle; also, the length of the perimeter of a circle.
Example:

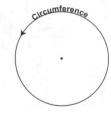

Commutative Property of Addition: Numbers can be added in any order and the sum will be the same.
Example: 3 + 4 = 4 + 3.

Commutative Property of Multiplication: Numbers can be multiplied in any order and the product will be the same.
Example: 3 x 6 = 6 x 3.

compare: To look for similarities and differences. For example, is one number greater than, less than, or equal to another number?

conclusion: A statement that follows logically from other facts.

Glossary

cone: A solid figure with a circle as its base and a curved surface that meets at a point.

cones

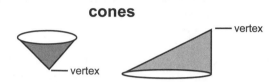

congruent figures: Figures that have the same shape and size.

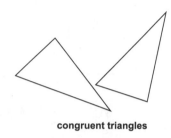

congruent triangles

cube: A solid figure with six faces that are congruent (equal) squares.

cylinder: A solid figure with two circular bases that are congruent (equal) and parallel to each other connected by a curved lateral surface.

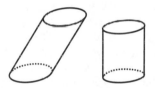

data: Information that is collected.

decimal number: A number expressed in base 10, such as 39,456, where each digit's value is determined by multiplying it by some power of 10.

denominator: The bottom number in a fraction.

diagram: A drawing that represents a mathematical situation.

difference: The answer when subtracting two numbers.

distance: The amount of space between two points.

dividend: A number in a division problem that is divided. Dividend ÷ divisor = quotient. Example: In 15 ÷ 3 = 5, 15 is the dividend.

$$\text{divisor}\overline{)\text{dividend}}^{\textstyle\text{quotient}} \qquad 3\overline{)15}^{\textstyle 5}$$

divisible: A number that can be divided by another number without leaving a remainder. Example: 12 is divisible by 3 because 12 ÷ 3 is an integer, namely 4.

division: An operation that tells how many equal groups there are or how many are in each group.

divisor: The number by which another number is divided. Example: In 15 ÷ 3 = 5, 3 is the divisor.

$$\text{divisor}\overline{)\text{dividend}}^{\textstyle\text{quotient}} \qquad 3\overline{)15}^{\textstyle 5}$$

edge: The line segment where two faces of a solid figure meet.

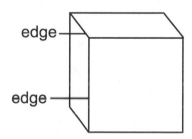

equivalent fractions: Two fractions with equal values.

equality: Two or more sets of values that are equal.

equation: A number sentence that says two expressions are equal (=). Example: 4 + 8 = 6 + 6.

estimate: To find an approximate value or measurement of something without exact calculation.

even number: A whole number that has a 0, 2, 4, 6, or 8 in the ones place. A number that is a multiple of 2. Examples: 0, 4, and 678 are even numbers.

expanded form: A number written as the sum of the values of its digits. Example: 546 = 500 + 40 + 6.

expression: A combination of variables, numbers, and symbols that represent a mathematical relationship.

Glossary

face: The sides of a solid figure. For example, a cube has six faces that are all squares. The pyramid below has five faces—four triangles and one square.

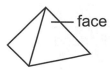

fact family: A group of related facts using the same numbers.
Example: 5 + 8 = 13; 13 − 8 = 5.

factor: One of two or more numbers that are multiplied together to give a product.
Example: In 4 x 3 = 12, 4 and 3 are factors of 12.

figure: A geometric figure is a set of points and/or lines in 2 or 3 dimensions.

flip (reflection): The change in a position of a figure that is the result of picking it up and turning it over.
Example: Reversing a "b" to a "d." Tipping a "p" to a "b" or a "b" to a "p" as shown below:

fraction: A symbol, such as $\frac{2}{8}$ or $\frac{5}{3}$, used to name a part of a whole, a part of a set, or a location on the number line.
Examples:

$$\frac{numerator}{denominator} = \frac{dividend}{divisor}$$

$$\frac{\text{\# of parts under consideration}}{\text{\# of parts in a set}}$$

function machine: Applies a function rule to a set of numbers, which determines a corresponding set of numbers.
Example: Input 9 ➡ Rule x 7 ➡ Output 63. If you apply the function rule "multiply by 7" to the values 5, 7, and 9, the corresponding values are:

5 ➡ 35
7 ➡ 49
9 ➡ 63

graph: A "picture" showing how certain facts are related to each other or how they compare to one another. Some examples of types of graphs are line graphs, pie charts, bar graphs, scatterplots, and pictographs.

grid: A pattern of regularly spaced horizontal and vertical lines on a plane that can be used to locate points and graph equations.

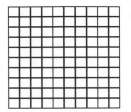

hexagon: A six-sided polygon. The total measure of the angles within a hexagon is 720°.

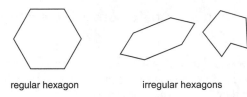

regular hexagon   irregular hexagons

impossible event: An event that can never happen.

integer: Any number, positive or negative, that is a whole number distance away from zero on a number line, in addition to zero. Specifically, an integer is any number in the set {. . .-3,-2,-1, 0, 1, 2, 3. . .}.
Examples of integers include: 1, 5, 273, -2, -35, and -1,375.

intersecting lines: Lines that cross at a point.
Examples:

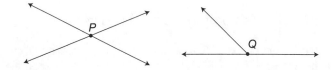

isosceles triangle: A triangle with at least two sides the same length.

justify: To prove or show to be true or valid using logic and/or evidence.

key: An explanation of what each symbol represents in a pictograph.

Glossary

kilometer (km): A metric unit of length: 1 kilometer = 1,000 meters.

line: A straight path of points that goes on forever in both directions.

line graph: A graph that uses a line or a curve to show how data changes over time.

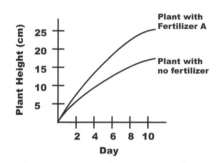

line of symmetry: A line on which a figure can be folded into two parts so that the parts match exactly.

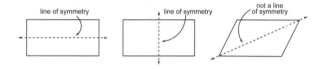

liter (L): A metric unit of capacity: 1 liter = 1,000 milliliters.

mass: The amount of matter an object has.

mean: Also called arithmetic average. A number found by adding two or more quantities together, and then dividing the sum by the number of quantities. For example, in the set {9, 5, 4} the mean is 6: 9 + 5 + 4 = 18; 18 ÷ 3 = 6. *See average.*

median: The middle number when numbers are put in order from least to greatest or from greatest to least. For example, in the set of numbers 6, 7, 8, 9, 10, the number 8 is the median (middle) number.

meter (m): A metric unit of length: 1 meter = 100 centimeters.

method: A systematic way of accomplishing a task.

mixed number: A number consisting of a whole number and a fraction.
Example: $6\frac{2}{3}$.

mode: The number or numbers that occur most often in a set of data. Example: The mode of {1, 3, 4, 5, 5, 7, 9} is 5.

multiple: A product of a number and any other whole number. Examples: {2, 4, 6, 8, 10, 12,…} are multiples of 2.

multiplication: An operation on two numbers that tells how many in all. The first number is the number of sets and the second number tells how many in each set.

number line: A line that shows numbers in order using a scale. Equal intervals are marked and usually labeled on the number line.

number sentence: An expression of a relationship between quantities as an equation or an inequality. Examples: 7 + 7 = 8 + 6; 14 < 92; 56 + 4 > 59.

numerator: The top number in a fraction.

octagon: An eight-sided polygon. The total measure of the angles within an octagon is 1080°.

odd number: A whole number that has 1, 3, 5, 7, or 9 in the ones place. An odd number is not divisible by 2. Examples: The numbers 53 and 701 are odd numbers.

operation: A mathematical process that combines numbers; basic operations of arithmetic include addition, subtraction, multiplication, and division.

order: To arrange numbers from the least to greatest or from the greatest to least.

ordered pair: Two numbers inside a set of parentheses separated by a comma that are used to name a point on a coordinate grid.

parallel lines: Lines in the same plane that never intersect.

parallelogram: A quadrilateral in which opposite sides are parallel.

pattern: An arrangement of numbers, pictures, etc., in an organized and predictable way. Examples: 3, 6, 9, 12, or ®0®0®0.

Glossary

pentagon: A five-sided polygon. The total measure of the angles within a pentagon is 540°.

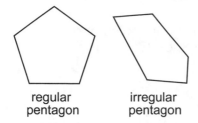

regular   irregular
pentagon   pentagon

perimeter: The distance around a figure.

perpendicular lines: Two lines that intersect to form a right angle (90 degrees).

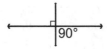

pictograph: A graph that uses pictures or symbols to represent similar data. The value of each picture is interpreted by a "key" or "legend."

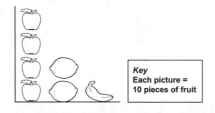

Key
Each picture =
10 pieces of fruit

place value: The value given to the place a digit has in a number.
Example: In the number 135, the 1 is in the hundreds place so it represents 100 (1 x 100); the 3 is in the tens place so it represents 30 (3 x 10); and the 5 is in the ones place so it represents 5 (5 x 1).

p.m.: The hours from noon to midnight; from the Latin words *post meridiem* meaning "after noon."

point: An exact position often marked by a dot.

polygon: A closed figure made up of straight line segments.

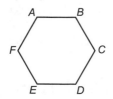

ABCDEF is a polygon.

possible event: An event that might or might not happen.

predict: To tell what you believe may happen in the future.

prediction: A prediction is a description of what may happen before it happens.

probability: The likelihood that something will happen.

product: The answer to a multiplication problem. Example: In 3 x 4 = 12, 12 is the product.

pyramid: A solid figure in which the base is a polygon and faces are triangles with a common point called a vertex.

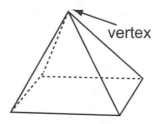

vertex

quadrilateral: A four-sided polygon. Rectangles, squares, parallelograms, rhombi, and trapezoids are all quadrilaterals. The total measure of the angles within a quadrilateral is 360°.
Example: *ABCD* is a quadrilateral.

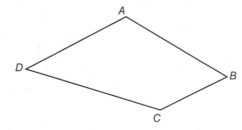

questionnaire: A set of questions for a survey.

quotient: The answer in a division problem.
Dividend ÷ divisor = quotient.
Example: In 15 ÷ 3 = 5, 5 is the quotient.

range: The difference between the least number and the greatest number in a data set. For example, in the set {4, 7, 10, 12, 36, 7, 2}, the range is 34; the greatest number (36) minus the least number (2): (36 – 2 = 34).

Glossary

rectangle: A quadrilateral with four right angles. A square is one example of a rectangle.

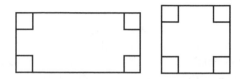

reflection: The change in the position of a figure that is the result of picking it up and turning it over. *See flip.*

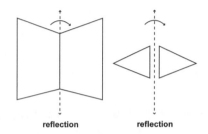

reflection   reflection

remainder: The number that is left over after dividing. Example: In 31 ÷ 7 = 4 R 3, the 3 is the remainder.

represent: To present clearly; describe; show.

rhombus: A quadrilateral with opposite sides parallel and all sides the same length. A square is one kind of rhombus.

right angle: An angle that forms a square corner and measures 90 degrees.

right triangle: A triangle having one right angle. *See right angle and triangle.*

rounding: Replacing an exact number with a number that tells about how much or how many to the nearest ten, hundred, thousand, and so on. Example: 52 rounded to the nearest 10 is 50.

rule: A procedure; a prescribed method; a way of describing the relationship between two sets of numbers. Example: In the following data, the rule is to add 3:

Input	Output
3	6
5	8
9	12

ruler: A straight-edged instrument used for measuring the lengths of objects. A ruler usually measures smaller units of length, such as inches or centimeters.

scale: The numbers that show the size of the units used on a graph.

sequence: A set of numbers arranged in a special order or pattern.

set: A group made up of numbers, figures, or parts.

side: A line segment connected to other segments to form the boundary of a polygon.

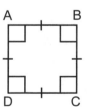

←side

similar: A description for figures that have the same shape.

slide (translation): The change in the position of a figure that moves up, down, or sideways. Example: scooting a book on a table.

solids: Figures in three dimensions.

solve: To find the solution to an equation or problem; finding the values of unknown variables that will make a true mathematical statement.

sphere: A solid figure in the shape of a ball. Example: a basketball is a sphere.

square: A rectangle with congruent (equal) sides. *See rectangle.*

square number: The product of a number multiplied by itself. Example: 49 is a square number (7 x 7 = 49).

square unit: A square with sides 1 unit long, used to measure area.

Glossary

standard form: A way to write a number showing only its digits. Example: 2,389.

standard units of measure: Units of measure commonly used; generally classified in the U.S. as the customary system or the metric system:

Customary System:
  Length
  1 foot (ft) = 12 inches (in)
  1 yard (yd) = 3 feet or 36 inches
  1 mile (mi) = 1,760 yards or 5,280 feet

  Weight
  16 ounces (oz) = 1 pound (lb)
  2,000 pounds = 1 ton (t)

  Capacity
  1 pint (pt) = 2 cups (c)
  1 quart (qt) = 2 pints
  1 gallon (gal) = 4 quarts

Metric System:
  Length
  1 centimeter (cm) = 10 millimeters (mm)
  1 decimeter (dm) = 10 centimeters
  1 meter (m) = 100 centimeters
  1 kilometer (km) = 1,000 meters

  Weight
  1,000 milligrams (mg) = 1 gram (g)
  1,000 grams (g) = 1 kilogram (kg)
  1,000 kilograms (kg) = 1 tonne (metric ton)

  Capacity
  1 liter (l) = 1,000 milliliters (ml)

strategy: A plan used in problem solving, such as looking for a pattern, drawing a diagram, working backward, etc.

subtraction: The operation that finds the difference between two numbers.

sum: The answer when adding two or more addends. Addend + Addend = Sum.

summary: A series of statements containing evidence, facts, and/or procedures that support a result.

survey: A way to collect data by asking a certain number of people the same question and recording their answers.

symmetry: A figure has line symmetry if it can be folded along a line so that both parts match exactly. A figure has radial or rotational symmetry if, after a rotation of less than 360°, it is indistinguishable from its former image.

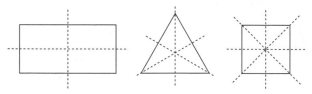
Examples of Figures With At Least Two Lines of Symmetry

table: A method of displaying data in rows and columns.

temperature: A measure of hot or cold in degrees.

translation (slide): A change in the position of a figure that moves it up, down, or sideways.

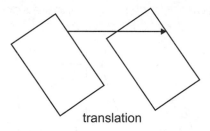
translation

triangle: A polygon with three sides. The sum of the angles of a triangle is always equal to 180°.

turn: The change in the position of a figure that moves it around a point. Also called a rotation.
Example: The hands of a clock turn around the center of the clock in a clockwise direction.

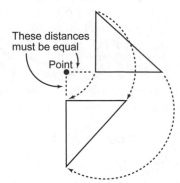
These distances must be equal
Point

Glossary

unlikely event: An event that probably will not happen.

vertex: The point where two rays meet to form an angle or where the sides of a polygon meet, or the point where 3 or more edges meet in a solid figure.

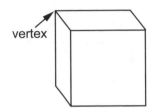

whole number: An integer in the set {0, 1, 2, 3 . . .}. In other words, a whole number is any number used when counting in addition to zero.

word forms: The number written in words. Examples: 546 is "five hundred forty-six."

Examples of Common Two-Dimensional Geometric Shapes

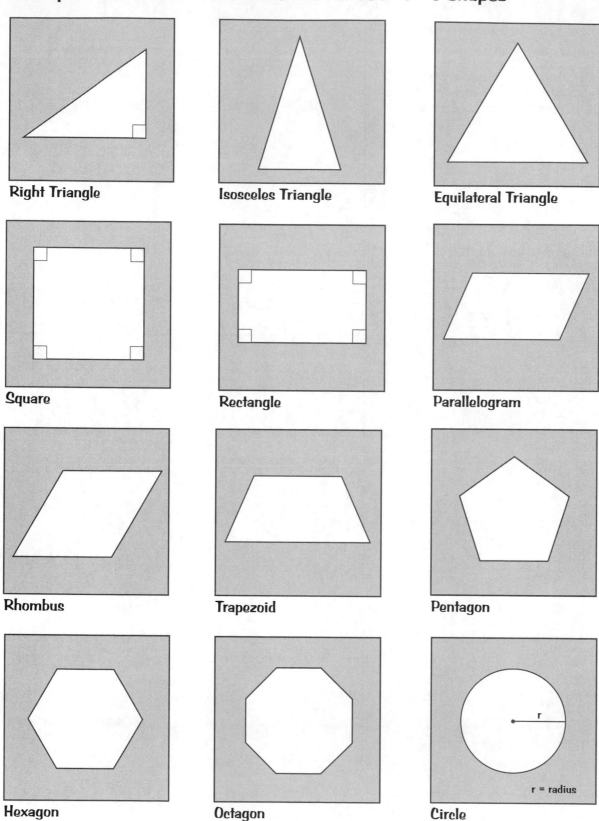

Examples of How Lines Interact

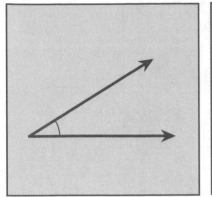

Acute Angle

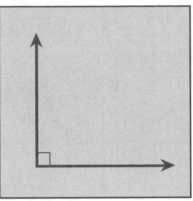

Right Angle

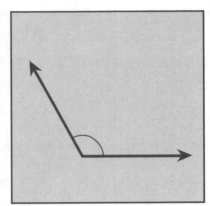

Obtuse Angle

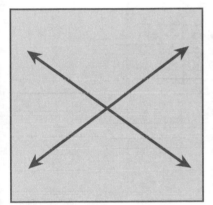

Intersecting

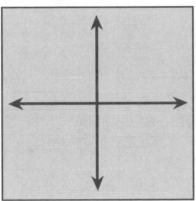

Perpendicular

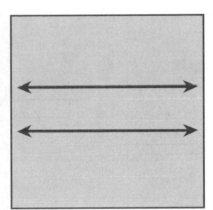

Parallel

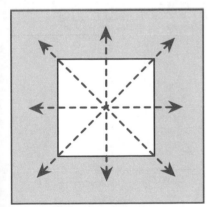

Lines of Symmetry

Examples of Common Types of Graphs

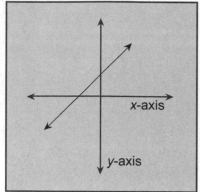

Line Graph

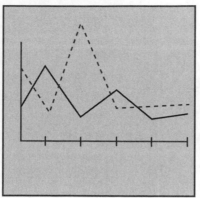

Double Line Graph

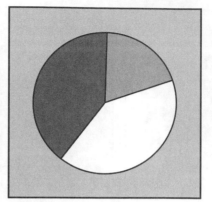

Pie Chart

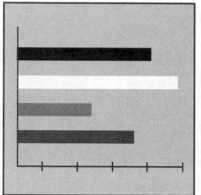

Bar Graph

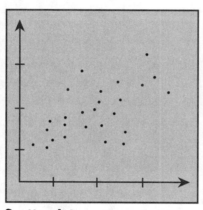

Scatterplot

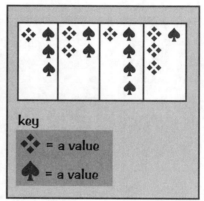

Pictograph

Examples of Common Three-Dimensional Objects

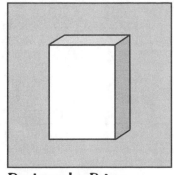

Cube

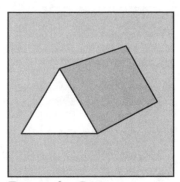

Rectangular Prism

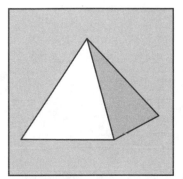

Triangular Prism

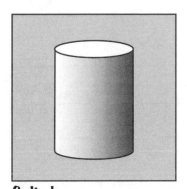

Pyramid

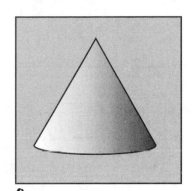

Cylinder

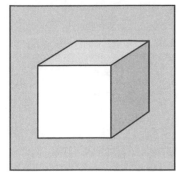

Cone

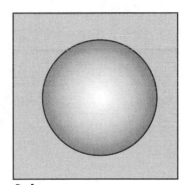

Sphere

Examples of Object Movement

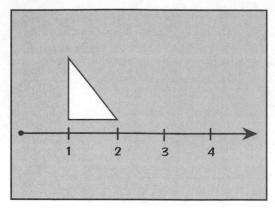 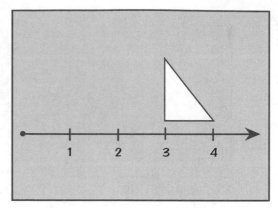

Translation

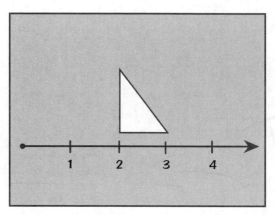 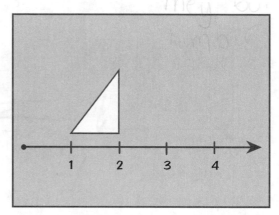

Reflection

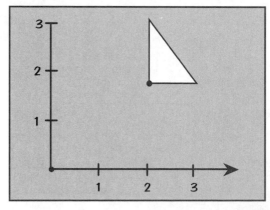 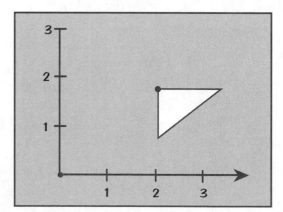

Rotation

Mathematics Assessment One

Directions for Taking the Mathematics Assessment

The Mathematics Assessment is made up of multiple-choice and short-answer questions. These questions show you how the skills you have learned in Mathematics class may be tested. The questions also give you a chance to practice your skills. If you have trouble with an area, talk with a parent or teacher.

Multiple-choice questions require you to pick the best answer out of four possible choices. Only one answer is correct. The short-answer questions will ask you to write your answer and explain your thinking using words, numbers, or pictures, or to show the steps you used to solve a problem. Remember to read the questions and the answer choices carefully. You will mark your answers on the answer document.

When you finish, check your answers.

1. Evaluate 12 × (6 + 2).

   A. 20

   B. 74

   C. 96

   D. 106

2. Mr. Wilson's class was having a pizza party. They ordered 5 large pizzas and 1 extra-large pizza. A large pizza has 8 pieces. An extra-large pizza has 12 pieces.

   Which number sentence can be used to find the total number of pieces of pizza Mr. Wilson's class ordered?

   A. 6 × 8

   B. (5 + 1) × 8

   C. 5 × 8 + 12

   D. (5 × 8) + 1

3. Look at the two number patterns below.

   Pattern Y: 8 13 18 23 28 33 38

   Pattern Z: 82 77 72 67 62 57 52

   What are the two missing numbers in Pattern Y? 8, 33

   What are the two missing numbers in Pattern Z? 72, 52

   Write **one** sentence that tells how Pattern Y and Pattern Z are similar.

   They both involve the number 5.

4. Jenna collected 1,547 pull tabs from soda cans for the school contest.

   What is the value of 5 in 1,547?

   A. 5

   B. 50

   C. 500

   D. 5000

Go On

5. Jose is making a small model of a statue he will put in the city park. The small model stands 5.625 inches tall. To make the actual statue he will enlarge the model by a scale factor of 100.

How tall will the actual statue be?

A. 56.25 in.

B. 562.5 in.

C. 5,625 in.

D. 56,250 in.

6. Which number is twenty and forty-five thousandths?

A. 0.2045

B. 20.45

C. 20.045

D. 2.045

7. George had four pet hamsters. He weighed them to see which was the biggest. The weights of the four hamsters are listed below.

5.06 oz; 5.61 oz; 5.6 oz; 5.006 oz

What is the order from **least** to **greatest** of the four weights?

A. 5.06 oz; 5.006 oz; 5.6 oz; 5.61 oz

B. 5.006 oz; 5.06 oz; 5.61 oz; 5.6 oz

C. 5.61 oz; 5.6 oz; 5.06 oz; 5.006 oz

D. 5.006 oz; 5.06 oz; 5.6 oz; 5.61 oz

Go On

8. Tim's mother gave him the grocery list below and asked him to buy all the items on it.

Bread $2.15   Milk $3.15   Cereal $3.60   2 Oranges at 69¢ each

Rounded to the nearest whole dollar, how much money should Tim take with him to the store?

A. $10.00

B. $11.00

C. $14.00

D. $20.00

Go On ▶

Copying is Prohibited   © Englefield & Associates, Inc.

9. A train is traveling at 36 miles per hour.

   How many miles would the train travel in 252 hours at this speed?

   A. 2,268

   B. 8,072

   C. 9,072

   D. 9,172

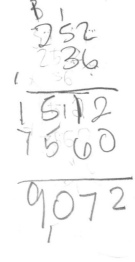

11. Look at the problem below.

    $1.3 + 2.47 = \square$

    What is the answer to the problem?

    A. 3.17

    B. 3.4

    C. 3.5

    D. 3.77

10. Jamal has a paper route and delivers the same amount of papers each week. Jamal delivered 9,828 newspapers in one year.

    How many newspapers did Jamal deliver each week?

    Show your work using words, numbers, or pictures.

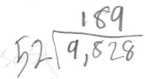

12. Kenna's mathematics teacher wrote this problem on the board.

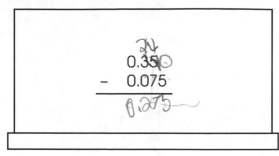

What is the difference between 0.35 and 0.075?

A. 0.275

B. 0.40

C. 0.285

D. 0.325

13. What is the sum of $12\frac{7}{8} + 11\frac{1}{6}$?

A. $23\frac{8}{14}$

B. $23\frac{4}{7}$

C. $23\frac{1}{24}$

D. $24\frac{1}{24}$

Go On

14. Ernie ate one-fourth of the cookies in the cookie jar. Julio ate one-third of the cookies in the cookie jar. Liv ate one-twelfth of the cookies in the cookie jar.

What fraction of the cookies were left in the cookie jar after Ernie, Julio, and Liv ate their cookies?

A. $\frac{1}{4}$

B. $\frac{1}{3}$

C. $\frac{2}{3}$

D. $\frac{3}{4}$

15. Lisa used 2 cups of sugar to make 3 pies.

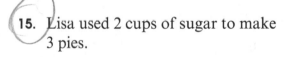

How much sugar did she use for each pie?

A. $\frac{1}{3}$ cup

B. $\frac{2}{3}$ cup

C. $1\frac{1}{3}$ cups

D. $1\frac{1}{2}$ cups

16. Gabe and Makenna have 60 books each. Gabe likes biographies more than Makenna. In Gabe's library, $\frac{3}{5}$ of his books are biographies and $\frac{1}{4}$ of Makenna's books are biographies.

How many biographies do they have altogether?

A. 15

B. 36

C. 51

D. 55

17. Two fractions which are both between 0 and 1 are multiplied together.

Which of the these statements is true?

A. The product will be less than either fraction.

B. The product will be greater than either fraction.

C. The product will be greater than one.

D. The product will be less than zero.

Go On

18. What is the product of $\frac{3}{4} \times \frac{2}{5}$ in simplest form?

    A. $\frac{3}{10}$

    B. $\frac{5}{19}$

    C. $\frac{3}{20}$

    D. $\frac{6}{20}$

19. Look at the number sentence.

$$15 \times \frac{1}{5} = 3$$

What other number sentence is **true**?

    A. $15 \div 3 = \frac{1}{5}$

    B. $15 \div \frac{1}{5} = 3$

    C. $3 \div \frac{1}{5} = 15$

    D. $\frac{1}{5} \div 3 = 15$

20. The Statue of Liberty is 151 feet 1 inch tall from base to torch.

How tall is the Statue of Liberty in inches?

    A. $12 \frac{2}{3}$ inches

    B. 454 inches

    C. 1812 inches

    D. 1813 inches

21. Wayne weighs 113 pounds.

How much does Wayne weigh in ounces?

1 pound = 16 ounces

    A. 1,808 ounces

    B. 1,130 ounces

    C. 70 ounces

    D. 7 ounces

Go On

22. The rectangular prism below is made of 1-inch cubes.

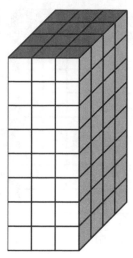

What is the volume of the rectangular prism?

A. 96 cubic inches

B. 84 cubic inches

C. 72 cubic inches

D. 56 cubic inches

23. Drew wants to know how much water his fish tank will hold.

What should Drew do?

A. measure the length, width, and height of the tank and find the area

B. measure the length and width of the sides to find the area

C. measure the height of the tank and multiply this by the width

D. measure the length, width, and height of the tank and find the volume

Go On ▶

24. A rectangular prism made of 1-inch cubes is shown below.

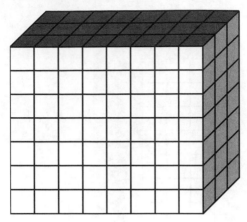

What is the volume of the rectangular prism?

A. 168 in.^{2}

B. 168 in.^{3}

C. 192 in.^{2}

D. 192 in.^{3}

Go On

25. On the grid below, what are the coordinates of Point *W*?

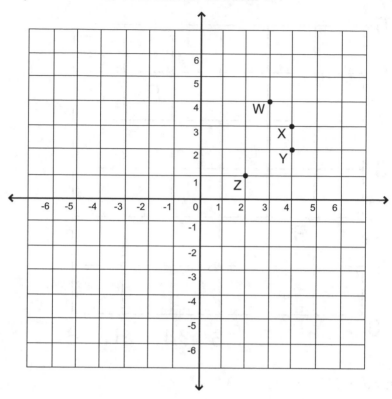

A. (4, 4)

B. (3, 4)

C. (3, 3)

D. (4, 3)

Go On ▶

26. Look at the graph below.

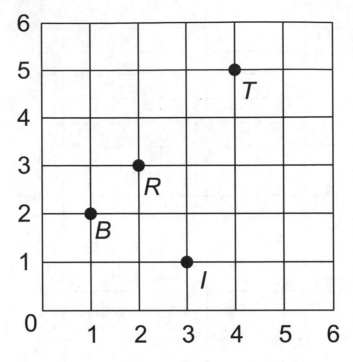

On the graph, which point is located at (2, 3)?

A. Point *B*

B. Point *I*

C. Point *R*

D. Point *T*

Go On

© Englefield & Associates, Inc.

27. Dexter made a map of his backyard on the coordinate grid shown below.

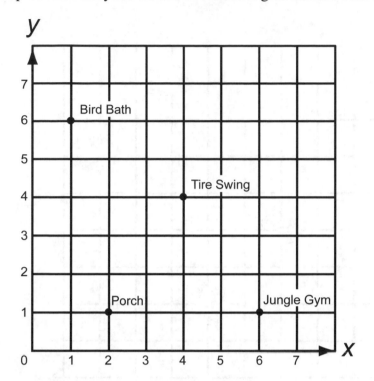

Which item listed below has the correct ordered pair?

A. Bird Bath; (6, 1)

B. Porch; (2, 1)

C. Tire Swing; (3, 3)

D. Jungle Gym (1, 6)

Go On

28. What are the coordinates for the boot?

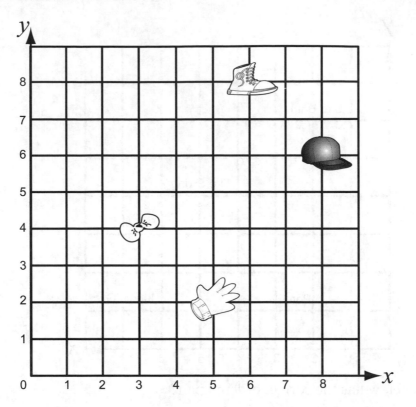

A. (5, 2)

B. (3, 4)

C. (6, 8)

D. (8, 6)

Go On ▶

29. Look at the Venn diagram below.

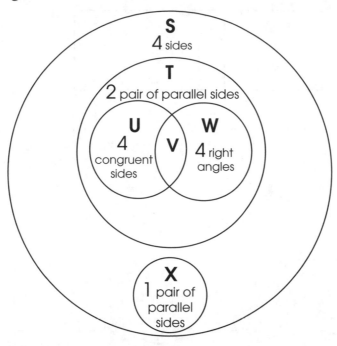

Which choice places the terms in the best location on diagram? Use the geometric properties associated with each term to help you decide.

A. S—quadrilateral; U—square; V—rhombus; X—trapezoid

B. T—rectangle; U—square; V—rhombus; X—trapezoid

C. S—quadrilateral; T—rectangle; V—square; X—trapezoid;

D. T—parallelogram; U—rhombus; V—square; W—rectangle

Go On ▶

30. Which of the following terms does NOT accurately describe the figures shown below?

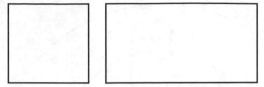

    A. polygon

    B. quadrilateral

    C. parallelogram

    D. trapezoid

31. For the end-of-the-year class party, Mr. Hernandez bought five gallons of ice cream, then decided to buy four more.

> 1 gallon = 16 cups

How many cups of ice cream did Mr. Hernandez buy?

    A. 128 cups

    B. 144 cups

    C. 576 cups

    D. 1,152 cups

Go On ▶

32. A rectangular prism made of 1-meter cubes is shown below.

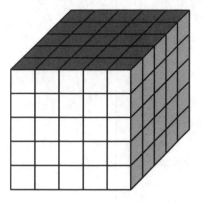

   What is the volume of the prism in cubic meters (m³)?

33. Mario wants to buy grapes. A sale sign in the window of Big Foods Grocery reads, "5 pounds of grapes, normally $4.65, now on sale for $3.95." Mario knows that Bob's Corner Store sells grapes for $0.72 a pound.

   Where should Mario buy 5 pounds of grapes if he wants to spend the least money possible?

   What would 3 pounds of grapes cost at Bob's Corner Store?

   Show or explain your work using words, numbers, and/or pictures.

Go On ▶

34. Compute the following.

$$\frac{4}{5} - \frac{1}{2} - \frac{1}{10}$$

 A. $\frac{2}{7}$

 B. $\frac{9}{10}$

 C. $\frac{3}{10}$

 D. $\frac{1}{5}$

35. Dan is learning the names of all the state capitals.

If he learns 6 names each day, how many days will it take him to learn the names of all 50 state capitals?

36. Lucy has 2 pounds of hamburger.

How many hamburgers can she make if each hamburger is $\frac{1}{3}$ pound?

Go On

37. Stephanie enters a one hour race for charity. Her family agrees to contribute a penny for every yard she runs during that hour.

If she runs 38,652 feet, how can she find out how many yards she ran?

A. She should multiply the number of feet she ran by 3.

B. She should divide the number of feet she ran by 3.

C. She should take the square root of the number of feet she ran.

D. It is impossible to convert feet into yards.

38. Lori and Theo are working on a report together. Lori has written $\frac{2}{3}$ of a page, and Theo has written $\frac{1}{6}$ of a page.

About how many pages have they written?

A. 1 page

B. 2 pages

C. 3 pages

D. 4 pages

Go On

39. Chang wants to buy a magazine. He has $10.00. He knows the magazine costs $4.95. When he buys the magazine, he is charged $0.28 in sales tax.

Which of the number sentences below can be used to find the amount of money Chang has after he buys the magazine?

A. $10.00 – $4.95

B. $10.00 – ($4.95 x $0.28)

C. $10.00 – $4.95 + $0.28

D. $10.00 – ($4.95 + $0.28)

40. Which of the following is equivalent to eleven thousand nineteen and five hundredths?

A. 11,019.500

B. 11,019.05

C. 1,119.05

D. 11,190.05

1 Ⓐ Ⓑ Ⓒ Ⓓ

2 Ⓐ Ⓑ Ⓒ Ⓓ

3

4 Ⓐ Ⓑ Ⓒ Ⓓ

5 Ⓐ Ⓑ Ⓒ Ⓓ

6 Ⓐ Ⓑ Ⓒ Ⓓ

7 Ⓐ Ⓑ Ⓒ Ⓓ

8 Ⓐ Ⓑ Ⓒ Ⓓ

9 Ⓐ Ⓑ Ⓒ Ⓓ

10

11 Ⓐ Ⓑ Ⓒ Ⓓ

12 Ⓐ Ⓑ Ⓒ Ⓓ

13 Ⓐ Ⓑ Ⓒ Ⓓ

14 Ⓐ Ⓑ Ⓒ Ⓓ

15 Ⓐ Ⓑ Ⓒ Ⓓ

16 Ⓐ Ⓑ Ⓒ Ⓓ

17 Ⓐ Ⓑ Ⓒ Ⓓ

18 Ⓐ Ⓑ Ⓒ Ⓓ

19 Ⓐ Ⓑ Ⓒ Ⓓ

20 Ⓐ Ⓑ Ⓒ Ⓓ

21 Ⓐ Ⓑ Ⓒ Ⓓ

22 Ⓐ Ⓑ Ⓒ Ⓓ

23 Ⓐ Ⓑ Ⓒ Ⓓ

24 Ⓐ Ⓑ Ⓒ Ⓓ

25 Ⓐ Ⓑ Ⓒ Ⓓ

26 Ⓐ Ⓑ Ⓒ Ⓓ

27 Ⓐ Ⓑ Ⓒ Ⓓ

28 Ⓐ Ⓑ Ⓒ Ⓓ

29 Ⓐ Ⓑ Ⓒ Ⓓ

30 Ⓐ Ⓑ Ⓒ Ⓓ

31 Ⓐ Ⓑ Ⓒ Ⓓ

32

33

34 Ⓐ Ⓑ Ⓒ Ⓓ

35

36

37 Ⓐ Ⓑ Ⓒ Ⓓ

38 Ⓐ Ⓑ Ⓒ Ⓓ

39 Ⓐ Ⓑ Ⓒ Ⓓ

40 Ⓐ Ⓑ Ⓒ Ⓓ

Mathematics Assessment Two

Directions for Taking the Mathematics Assessment

The Mathematics Assessment is made up of multiple-choice and short-answer questions. These questions show you how the skills you have learned in Mathematics class may be tested. The questions also give you a chance to practice your skills. If you have trouble with an area, talk with a parent or teacher.

Multiple-choice questions require you to pick the best answer out of four possible choices. Only one answer is correct. The short-answer questions will ask you to write your answer and explain your thinking using words, numbers, or pictures, or to show the steps you used to solve a problem. Remember to read the questions and the answer choices carefully. You will mark your answers on the answer document.

When you finish, check your answers.

1. Evaluate the following equation.

$$50 - (8 \times 6)$$

A. 2

B. 4

C. 98

D. 432

2. Every year the town of Mallard has a rubber ducky race in the river. In this year's race, 23 people entered 3 rubber duckies, 57 people entered 2 rubber duckies, and 106 people entered 1 rubber ducky.

Which number sentence below can be used to find the total number of rubber duckies in the race?

A. $(23 + 57 + 106) \times (3 + 2 + 1)$

B. $(23 + 57 + 106) \times (3 \times 2 \times 1)$

C. $(23 + 57 + 106) \times 2$

D. $(23 \times 3) + (57 \times 2) + 106$

3. Look at the two number patterns below.

Pattern Y: ☐ 4 6 8 10 ☐ 14

Pattern Z: 4 8 12 ☐ 20 24 ☐

What are the two missing numbers in Pattern Y?

What are the two missing numbers in Pattern Z?

Write one sentence that tells how Pattern Y and Pattern Z are related.

4. What is the value of the 3 in the number 37,902?

A. 3

B. 3×100

C. $3 \times 1,000$

D. $3 \times 10,000$

Go On ▶

5. A photocopy store charges $0.10 per copy.

    How much does it cost to make 500 copies?

    A. $0.50

    B. $5.00

    C. $50.00

    D. $5,000.00

6. The fastest speed reached by a jet during a flight was three hundred twenty-nine and twenty-four hundredths. The jet's speed is given in miles per hour.

    Which of the following describes the fastest speed of the jet?

    A. 320.924 miles per hour

    B. 329.024 miles per hour

    C. 329.24 miles per hour

    D. 329.204 miles per hour

7. Harvey and his friends entered their pet snails in the 17th Annual Snail Race. The speeds of their snails are listed in miles per hour in the table below.

Snail	Speed (mph)
Bing	0.031
Slimy	0.029
Gunga	0.04
Roxie	0.009

    Which snail is the fastest?

    A. Bing

    B. Slimy

    C. Gunga

    D. Roxie

Go On

8. Yvonne stopped by the grocery store after work to pick up a few items. She mentally added the costs of her items as she shopped.

Item	Price
Milk	$3.19
Cheese	$3.79
Bread	$2.09
Ice Cream	$4.09
Eggs	$1.80

When she got to the register, about how much did she expect to pay?

A. $13.00

B. $15.00

C. $18.00

D. $20.00

9. If Jerry delivers 269 newspapers a week, how many newspapers does he deliver in a year?

A. 13,478 newspapers

B. 13,878 newspapers

C. 13,978 newspapers

D. 13,988 newspapers

10. A large piñata was brought in for a class party. The piñata was filled with 841 pieces of candy.

If each of the 29 students in the class got the same amount of candy, how many pieces of candy did each student receive?

11. Look at the problem.

$$0.71 + 0.53 = \square$$

What is the correct answer to the problem?

A. 0.18

B. 0.24

C. 1.18

D. 1.24

Go On▶

12. Look at the problem below.

$$1.31 - 0.89 = \square$$

What is the correct answer to the problem?

A. 0.42

B. 0.52

C. 1.2

D. 2.2

13. The models below represent two different fractions.

$\frac{1}{2}$  =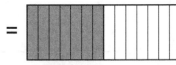

$\frac{3}{7}$  =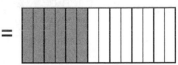

Which equation below shows the sum of these two fractions?

A. $\frac{1}{2} + \frac{3}{7} = \frac{13}{14}$

B. $\frac{1}{2} + \frac{3}{7} = \frac{4}{9}$

C. $\frac{1}{2} + \frac{3}{7} = \frac{4}{14}$

D. $\frac{1}{2} + \frac{3}{7} = 1\frac{1}{14}$

Go On

14. Freddy, Gina, and Oscar are putting together a puzzle. So far, Freddy has put together five-sixteenths of the puzzle, Gina has put together one-fourth of the puzzle, and Oscar has put together three-eighths of the puzzle.

Which expression can be used to find out how much of the puzzle is not put together?

A. $\frac{16}{16} - (\frac{5}{16} + \frac{4}{16} + \frac{6}{16})$

B. $\frac{16}{16} - \frac{5}{16} + \frac{4}{16} + \frac{6}{16}$

C. $\frac{16}{16} - (\frac{5}{16} - \frac{4}{16} - \frac{6}{16})$

D. $\frac{5}{16} + \frac{4}{16} + \frac{6}{16}$

15. Five people want to share 4 pounds of fudge equally.

How many pounds of fudge will each person get?

A. $\frac{4}{5}$ pound

B. 1 pound

C. $1\frac{1}{5}$ pounds

D. $2\frac{1}{2}$ pounds

Go On

16. Look at the business card shown below.

one square = one inch

What is the area of the business card?

A. 7 square inches

B. 8 square inches

C. 10 square inches

D. 11 square inches

17. Julie wants to resize a photo so that it is $\frac{5}{2}$ times the size of the original photo.

Which statement is true?

A. The new photo will be larger than the original photo.

B. The new photo will be smaller than the original photo.

C. The new photo will be about the same size as the original photo.

D. The new photo will be about 5 times the size of the original photo.

Go On

18. What is the product of $\frac{1}{6} \times \frac{3}{4}$ in simplest form?

   A. $\frac{1}{8}$

   B. $\frac{3}{10}$

   C. $\frac{1}{24}$

   D. $\frac{3}{24}$

19. Look at the number sentence.

$$18 \times \frac{1}{3} = 6$$

What other number sentence is **true**?

   A. $18 \div 6 = \frac{1}{3}$

   B. $18 \div \frac{1}{6} = 3$

   C. $6 \div \frac{1}{3} = 18$

   D. $\frac{1}{3} \div 6 = 18$

20. Kareem is building a model of a monument. The monument is 3 times as tall as it is wide.

   If the monument is 396 inches tall, what is the width of the monument in feet?

   A. 11 feet

   B. 33 feet

   C. 99 feet

   D. 132 feet

21. The Liberty Bell weighs about 2,080 pounds.

   | 1 pound = 16 ounces |

   About how many ounces does the Liberty Bell weigh?

   A. 33,280 ounces

   B. 26,000 ounces

   C. 16,640 ounces

   D. 13,000 ounces

Go On ▶

22. Cara is making a set of building blocks for her little niece. Each block is a one inch cube. She built the box below to store the blocks.

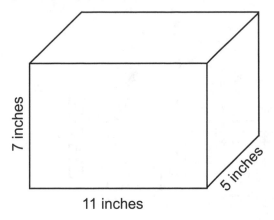

How many blocks will fit into the storage box?

A. 385

B. 334

C. 279

D. 77

23. Terry says his container holds 2.5 liters of juice.

What does this measurement represent?

A. volume

B. area

C. height

D. perimeter

Go On

24. Keenan wants to fill the flower box below with soil.

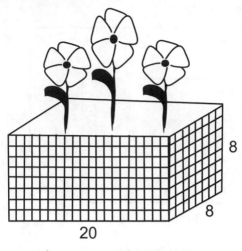

8

8

20

1 square = 1 inch

About how much soil will Keenan need to fill the box to the top with soil?

A. 1280 cubic inches

B. 640 cubic inches

C. 512 cubic inches

D. 160 cubic inches

Go On

25. What are the coordinates of point *N* on the grid below?

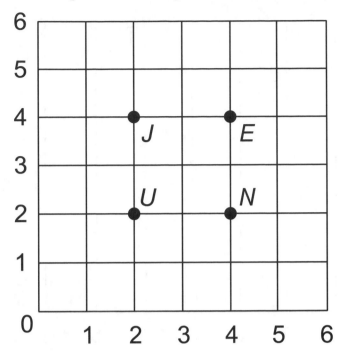

A. (2, 2)

B. (4, 4)

C. (4, 2)

D. (2, 4)

Go On ▶

26. On the grid below, which point is located at the coordinates (1, 5)?

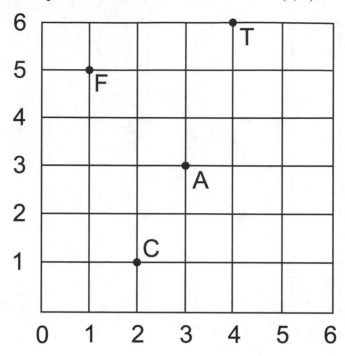

A. Point A

B. Point C

C. Point F

D. Point T

© Englefield & Associates, Inc.

Go On

27. Which animal is located at (5, 2) on the grid below?

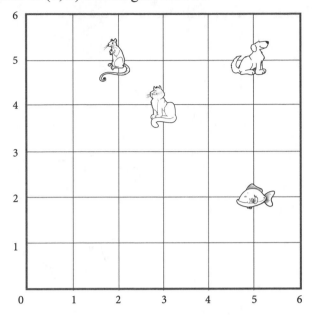

A. cat

B. mouse

C. fish

D. dog

Go On ▶

28. Below is a map of Gerald's backyard. Each box on the grid measures 1 square yard. For his brother's pirate party, he has buried some things in the places shown on the map.

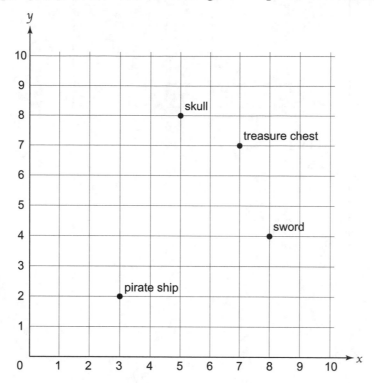

What are the coordinates for the pirate ship?

A. (2, 3)

B. (3, 2)

C. (7, 7)

D. (8, 4)

Go On

29. Baily's class was shown a figure and asked to describe it.

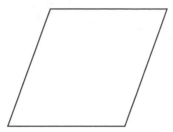

Which list of terms describes this figure?

A. Parallelogram, rhombus, square

B. Quadrilateral, parallelogram, rhombus

C. Quadrilateral, rectangle, square

D. Quadrilateral, rhombus, square

30. What type of figures is shown below?

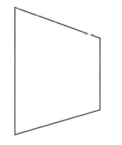 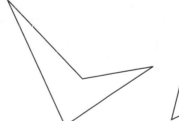  

A. quadrilaterals

B. squares

C. triangles

D. parallelograms

Go On

31. For the end-of-the-year class party, Mr. Hernandez bought 9 gallons of ice cream.

> 16 cups = 1 gallon

How many cups of ice cream did Mr. Hernandez buy?

A. 128 cups

B. 144 cups

C. 576 cups

D. 1,152 cups

32. A rectangular prism made of 1-mile cubes is shown below.

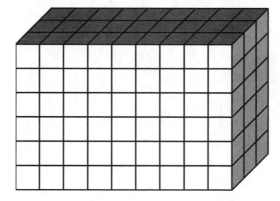

What is the volume of the prism in cubic miles?

Go On ▶

33. Ismail is buying fruit at the local market. He wants to buy 2.5 lbs of bananas, which are priced at $1.44 per pound.

How much will he pay for the bananas?

35. Solve: $3(\frac{1}{2} - \frac{1}{8})$.

Show your work.

36. How many $\frac{1}{2}$-cup servings are in 3 cups of milk?

Show your work.

34. Kathy has 578 seashells that she collected during 17 trips to the ocean. Kathy collected the same amount of shells each trip.

How many seashells did Kathy collect on each trip?

A. 24

B. 34

C. 35

D. 30

Go On ▶

37. Look at the model.

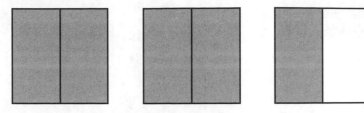

Which fraction does the shaded areas represent?

A. $\frac{5}{2}$

B. $\frac{5}{6}$

C. $\frac{3}{2}$

D. $\frac{3}{6}$

38. Ursula and Sharon were baking cookies. They baked a total of 18 dozen cookies. They took 100 cookies to their teachers. They gave 84 cookies away to friends. Their friend, Maggie, gave Ursula and Sharon 10 cookies each.

> 1 dozen = 12 cookies

Which number sentence could be used to find the total number of cookies Ursula and Sharon have now?

A. $(18 \times 12) - 100 - 84 + 10$

B. $(18 \times 12) - 100 - 84 + (2 \times 10)$

C. $(18 - 100 + 84 + 10) \times 12$

D. $(18 \times 12) - (100 + 84 + 10)$

Go On

39. Reese was making a poster for her room. She wanted the poster to be a parallelogram other than a square or rectangle.

What could her poster look like?

A.

B.

C.

D.

Go On ▶

40. Which of the following numbers is three hundred four thousand and fifty-two thousandths?

   A. 304,000.52

   B. 304,000.052

   C. 304,000.0052

   D. 3,004,000.0052

1 Ⓐ Ⓑ Ⓒ Ⓓ

2 Ⓐ Ⓑ Ⓒ Ⓓ

3

4 Ⓐ Ⓑ Ⓒ Ⓓ

5 Ⓐ Ⓑ Ⓒ Ⓓ

6 Ⓐ Ⓑ Ⓒ Ⓓ

7 Ⓐ Ⓑ Ⓒ Ⓓ

8 Ⓐ Ⓑ Ⓒ Ⓓ

9 Ⓐ Ⓑ Ⓒ Ⓓ

10

11 Ⓐ Ⓑ Ⓒ Ⓓ

12 Ⓐ Ⓑ Ⓒ Ⓓ

13 Ⓐ Ⓑ Ⓒ Ⓓ

14 Ⓐ Ⓑ Ⓒ Ⓓ

15 Ⓐ Ⓑ Ⓒ Ⓓ

16 Ⓐ Ⓑ Ⓒ Ⓓ

17 Ⓐ Ⓑ Ⓒ Ⓓ

18 Ⓐ Ⓑ Ⓒ Ⓓ

19 Ⓐ Ⓑ Ⓒ Ⓓ

20 Ⓐ Ⓑ Ⓒ Ⓓ

21 Ⓐ Ⓑ Ⓒ Ⓓ

22 Ⓐ Ⓑ Ⓒ Ⓓ

23 Ⓐ Ⓑ Ⓒ Ⓓ

24 Ⓐ Ⓑ Ⓒ Ⓓ

25 Ⓐ Ⓑ Ⓒ Ⓓ

26 Ⓐ Ⓑ Ⓒ Ⓓ

27 Ⓐ Ⓑ Ⓒ Ⓓ

28 Ⓐ Ⓑ Ⓒ Ⓓ

29 Ⓐ Ⓑ Ⓒ Ⓓ

30 Ⓐ Ⓑ Ⓒ Ⓓ

31 Ⓐ Ⓑ Ⓒ Ⓓ

32

33

34 Ⓐ Ⓑ Ⓒ Ⓓ

35

36

37 Ⓐ Ⓑ Ⓒ Ⓓ

38 Ⓐ Ⓑ Ⓒ Ⓓ

39 Ⓐ Ⓑ Ⓒ Ⓓ

40 Ⓐ Ⓑ Ⓒ Ⓓ

Notes

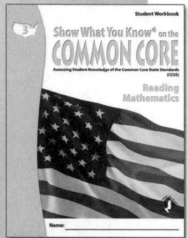